Wales Walking

Contents

*Only walks inside Wales are featured

All information in this booklet is grouped under the main Ordnance Survey 1:50,000 series map sheets on which they appear. A further simple locating map is provided.

This Wales Tourist Board publication is distributed overseas by the British Tourist Authority, which maintains offices in 19 countries, as well as in London where prospective visitors to Britain may obtain Tourist information. Consult your Telephone Directory in Amsterdam; Brussels; Buenos Aires; Capetown; Chicago; Copenhagen; Dallas; Frankfurt; Johannesburg; London; Los Angeles; Madrid; Melbourne; Mexico City; New York; Oslo; Paris; Rome; Sao Paulo; Stockholm; Sydney; Tokyo; Toronto; Vancouver; Wellington: Zurich. (see page 99).

Introduction

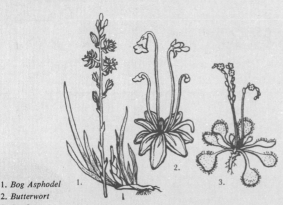

1. *Bog Asphodel*
2. *Butterwort*
3. *Sundew*
Flowers found in Snowdonia National Park.

This list of Nature and Town Trails, Forest Walks and related facilities has been compiled by the Wales Tourist Board from information prepared by the major organisations in Wales.

Your enjoyment of the countryside has been uppermost in their thoughts. At the same time they hope that every thought and consideration will be given by the walker to the countryside, its birds, animals and plants, and particularly to the people to whom the land is a workshop. Follow the suggestions of the Country Code and you will be well received.

The organisations responsible have prepared a special brochure or booklet for most of the walks and trails. They can be bought at the start of the walk from 'Honesty Boxes', at some information centres, or obtained in advance from the organisations mentioned in each walk. Addresses of these organisations are given at the back of the book.

Unwaymarked rambles have been prepared mainly with the co-operation of the Ramblers Association Welsh Council; The Wales Tourist Board acknowledges the great assistance provided by the Council.

The Wales Tourist Board would be glad to have your views on the walks and trails, particularly on aspects of their layout and description in this book. **Send them to the Wales Tourist Board, High Street, Llandaff, Cardiff CF5 2YZ.**

Symbols:

Access information:

- ▯ Limited car park nearby
- ▤ Railway station nearby
- ⊕ Bus route nearby

Walk is suitable for:

A Family parties in casual clothes
B Energetic types well shod
C Fit enthusiasts fully equipped

Walk is in an area of:

1 Cliffs and sunny screes
2 Duneland, estuary banks or foreshore
3 Wetlands and river, canal, lake or reservoir banks
4 Meadow, hay and cornfields, hedges, walls, grassy banks, roadsides, gardens and parks
5 Woodlands, forests and shady places
6 Hillsides, moorland, heath and mountain
7 Architectural and historic interest

R.U.P.P. Road used as a public path

Walks numbered in the upright bold print style are waymarked or described by leaflet or booklet. Those marked in italics are non-waymarked rambles (see page 7).

The maps used in this book are based on the Wales Tourist Board's map at 5 miles – 1 inch. Copyright © Wales Tourist Board, 1978.

Acknowledgements

The Wales Tourist Board wishes to thank the following people and organisations for their help in providing information and checking information in this booklet:

County, Borough and District Councils of Wales.
Countryside Commission.
Forestry Commission.
National Park Officers: Snowdonia, Brecon Beacons, Pembrokeshire Coast.
National Trust.
Naturalists' Trusts in Wales.
Nature Conservancy.
Offas Dyke Association:
Ramblers' Association Welsh Council.
Mr. R. B. Rowson, Cardiff.
Royal Society for the Protection of Birds.
Water Space Amenity Commission for information on bird watching at reservoirs in Wales.
Mr. Ernie Way, Guildford.
Illustrations by John Barber.

Every effort has been made to ensure accuracy in this publication but the Wales Tourist Board can accept no liability for any inaccuracies or omissions.

Extensive reference is made in this book to land, paths, road access points and installations which may or may not be on private property. Such quotations or mention herein do not imply a right of way or any other rights and walkers should take care to see that the necessary permissions in the proper form are always obtained from the owners or their agents before use is made of such facilities. The Wales Tourist Board gives no representation warranty or guarantee regarding the right to use the land, paths, road access points and installations and accepts no liability whatsoever in respect thereof.

Leaflets and Brochures on Trails and Walks

Detailed leaflets to each walk, where published, can be obtained from the nearest Tourist Information Centre or from organizations mentioned in each entry on sending the money and foolscap or A4 size stamped and addressed envelope. Their addresses are listed at the back of this booklet.

Maps

The map sheet numbers of the Ordnance Survey referred to in this Guide are in the 1 : 50,000 scale series published by the Ordnance Survey, available from H.M. Stationery Office, shops and many bookshops.

In some areas, particularly parts of the National Parks and areas designated as of outstanding natural beauty, walkers will be better served by the 'Outdoor Leisure Maps' series of the Ordnance Survey at 1 : 25,000 scale.

Picnic Sites

Many walks and trails have picnic sites as their starting point or one may be provided at some particularly convenient and restful spot on the route of the walk. Many more are provided for motorists, but all have one thing in common; almost invariably they give an opportunity for rambles and walks in their immediate vicinity.

The Country Code

The Country Code issued by the Countryside Commission lists ten points which, if strictly adhered to at all times, would go a long way to making your visit an enjoyable one. So, please,

- Guard against all risk of fire.
- Fasten all gates.
- Keep dogs under proper control.
- Keep to the rights of way across farm land.
- Avoid damaging farms, hedges and walls.
- Leave no litter.

- Safeguard water supplies.
- Protect wildlife, wild plants and trees.
- Go carefully on country roads and, particularly if there is no car park, please do not block the road so that local people cannot get about, nor use a a convenient field for parking.
- Respect the life of the countryside.

Grading of walks

All walks in the Nature Trail and Forest Walk sections, which are mainly waymarked or covered by a guide book, have been graded according to their suitability for:
Family parties: The walk is suitable for older people and the young who may not be used to lengthy walks in the countryside.
Energetic types: Fit people of any age can undertake these walks.
Fit enthusiasts: These walks are for the fit in both sexes – physically fit and accomplished in orienteering or in near potentially dangerous terrain under weather conditions that might turn for the worst.

On walks where waymarking is the exception, walks up to 8 miles long are generally considered suitable for energetic types but beyond that distance, or where difficult moorland or mountain terrain has to be traversed, walks should only be attempted by fit enthusiasts or in their company.

Roads used as Public Paths – R.U.P.P.

The initials R.U.P.P. are used occasionally in this book and denote certain roads which are used as public paths.

Forestry Commission land

Visitors are invited to walk along paths in the Commission's forests provided cars are parked outside the forests in officially recognised car parks or in positions where no obstruction is caused. No fires should be lit and care should be taken at all times to avoid causing fires accidentally, or to cause damage to fences and trees.

Walking holidays and activities in the countryside

Tariffs will be supplied on application.

(**For accommodation at other places in Wales ask at Tourist Information Centres for the publication 'Where to Stay in Wales', price 50p, or send direct to The Wales Tourist Board, Llandaff, Cardiff.**)

Brecon Beacons National Park

Study Centre, Danywenallt, Talybont-on-Usk, nr. Brecon

Danywenallt is a small centre created from a derelict farmhouse and barn. As its name indicates, it stands 'below the fair wooded hillside' about 1½ miles up the Caerfanell valley south of Talybont-on-Usk.

The purpose of the centre is to provide opportunity for study in depth of the Brecon Beacons National Park – and of its constituent elements.

There is a lecture room, small reference library and some basic equipment. Everyone is asked to give some help with domestic routines, as far as courses allow. By these means it is possible to keep fees at a modest level.

Courses include natural history, flowers, exploring, planning, landscape painting, trees and teacher's weekends.
Enquiries about the courses and use of the centre should be addressed to the National Park Officer, Glamorgan Street, Brecon, Powys LD3 7DP (Brecon 2311 and 3378).

Field Studies Council

Rhyd-y-Creuau

The Drapers, Field Centre, Betws-y-Coed, Gwynedd Tel. *Betws-y-Coed* 494. (**Enquiries to Warden**)

Accommodation in single or double rooms and a 7 bed dormitory. Breakfast, dinner and evening snack are taken at the centre, packed lunch is provided every day, special diets available. Open all year. Courses include: Drawing, mosses, birds, mountain weather, mountain structure and life, history, plant life, art, photography and recreation planning.

Dalefort Field Centre

Haverfordwest, Dyfed
Tel. Dale 205

Courses include: Geology, bird watching, photography, biology and painting. Individuals and groups up to maximum of 65.

Orielton Field Centre,

Pembroke, Dyfed
Tel. Castlemartin 225

Courses include: Bird watching, illustration, shell life, lichens. Individuals and groups up to 70 taken.

Jesse James Bunkhouse

Buarth-y-Clytiau, Penisarwaen,
Llanberis, Gwynedd
Tel. Llanberis 521. (**Enquiries to:** J. James)

Accommodation in a bunk-house, an annex, a flat and house sleeping a total of 45. The accommodation is mainly self-catering though meals can be provided by arrangement. Activities include rock climbing, hill walking, canoeing and pony riding. Equipment for hire.

Minerva Outdoor Ventures

Crown House, 19 London Road,
High Wycombe, Bucks.
Tel. High Wycombe 29927

Based on Penyrheol Adventure Centre in southern foothills of Black Mountain near Ystradgynlais, Swansea Valley.

Adventure Holidays – Canoeing and sailing, rock climbing, hill walking, caving, pony trekking, and general interests for children over 9 years of age.

Geographical Field Study courses for students. Elementary mountain craft, fulfilling the Mountain Leadership Certificate requirements.

Plas-y-Brenin National Mountaineering Centre

Capel Curig, Betws-y-Coed,
Gwynedd
Tel. Capel Curig 214/280. (**Enquiries** to J. A. Jackson)

Accommodation in two and three bedded rooms. Courses include mountain climbing, geography, photography and rescue, canoeing and fishing. Special facilities include an artificial ski slope and training track and an outdoor heated swimming pool.

Plas-y-Brenin, Mountaineering Centre of the Central Council for Physical Recreation at Capel Curig in Snowdonia.

Snowdonia National Park Studies Centre

Plas Tan-y-Bwlch, Maentwrog,
Gwynedd
Tel. Maentwrog 324/334. (**Enquiries to: Mr. A. E. J. Buckhurst**)

Plas Tan-y-Bwlch is a modern-ised mansion with accommodation for 54 people (individuals and groups), mostly in single and double rooms. Courses of various aspects for the general public, 'A' level courses for biologists and geographers, and courses for in-service teachers and specialist groups. The Centre is also available for independent groups to pursue their own programme.

Tan Troed Adventure Centre

Brecon Beacons National Park,
Powys
(**Enquiries to: P. G. L., Young Adventure Ltd., 50-100 Station Street, Ross-on-Wye, Hereford-shire HR9 7AH. Tel. Ross-on-Wye 4211/7**)

Accommodation for 200 young people provided in purpose-built units. A choice of holidays is available, at fully inclusive prices, for children aged 9–11 and young

people aged 12–15 and 16–25 including sailing, pony trekking, canoeing, combined with caving, archery, long-boat canal cruising, cycling, hill-walking, orienteering. All equipment is provided.

The Christian Mountain Centre

Gorffwysfa, Tremadog, Gwynedd
Tel. Portmadoc 2616. (**Enquiries to: The Warden**)

Courses in mountain walking, camping and canoeing, climbing, mountain leadership, environ-mental studies, horse riding, oil painting. Equipment supplied. Accommodates 30 plus 2 leaders/ teachers.

The Country-Wide Holidays Association

Birch Heys, Cromwell Range,
Manchester M14 6HU
Tel. 061-224 2887/8

Holidays based at Llanfair-fechan, Barmouth and Lampeter, designed mainly to encourage an appreciation of the countryside through walking and/or climbing. Holidays for young people, photography, canoeing and rock climbing activities also available.

The Holiday Fellowship Ltd.

(Enquiries to: The Manager, The Holiday Fellowship Ltd., 142 Great North Way, Hendon, London NW4 1EG Tel. 01-2033381).

Holiday Fellowship

Penscoed Youth Camp, Devils Bridge, Aberystwyth, Dyfed.

Accommodation for 71 plus 8 leaders, camp style with double bunks arranged in small groups in chalets. One large room for dining, recreation and study. Open March to end of September. Age range 8–18 years. Centre particularly suitable for varied field courses.

Holiday Fellowship

The Priory Youth Guest House, Llandogo, Gwent Tel. St. Briavel's 675

Accommodation for 100 plus leaders. Open all year. Age range 8–18 years. Moderate size house, with additional accommodation in a cottage and garden houses. Priory overlooking River Wye.

Holiday Fellowship

Bryn Dinas Youth Guest House, Nantgwynant, Gwynedd

Accommodation for 50, double bunks in dormitories. Open March to September. Age range 8–18 years.

Holiday Fellowship

Tregoyd Guest House, Three Cocks, Powys Tel. Glasbury 375

Guest House accommodation. Open March to September. Group booking of up to 66 approximately accepted. Individuals also accepted. Advance booking necessary.

The Nurtons Field Centre

Tintern, Chepstow, Gwent Tel. 253

Week and weekend courses on various aspects of the countryside. Individuals and groups up to 14 in number.

Trehaidd Field Centre

Brynberian, Crymych, Dyfed
(Enquiries to: Miss R. J. Conran, 14 Milton Court, Parkleys, Ham, Richmond, Surrey. Tel. 01–546 7471), or Dr. and Mrs. O. F. Conran, Tycanol Farm, Brynberian, Crymych, Dyfed. Tel. Crosswell (023 979) 282

Self-catering farmhouse, sleeps 15. Open all year. Visitors to Trehaidd have access to Tycanol, a neighbouring farm, whose maritime woodland is a nature reserve and is a particularly good base for studies in marine biology.

Some useful books on Walking in Wales not otherwise mentioned under specific walks

	Author	Published by	Price
Idwal Log		Y.H.A.	15p
Berwyn Log		Y.H.A.	15p
Elenith	Timothy Porter	Y.H.A.	15p
Exploring the Wye Valley	Roger Jones	Harvey Barton, Bristol	40p
Walks in the Taff Valley	David Rees	The Starling Press, Tredegar Street, Risca, Gwent	90p
Thirty walks in Gower	Roger Jones	Roger Jones, Green Close, Llanmorlais, West Glam. SA4 3TL	25p
Ten walks in Gower	Stephen Rees	Gower Society, Royal Institution, Victoria Street, Swansea	10p
Four walks in Gower		Glamorgan Naturalists' Trust, c/o Pengwern, Llanblethian, Cowbridge	15p (plus 10p postage and packing)
Ffestiniog Log	Kathleen Austin	Y.H.A.	15p
Hill walking in Snowdonia	E. G. Rowland	Cicerone Press, 16 Briarsfield Road, Warsley, Manchester	75p
Welsh Walks and Legends	Showell Styles	John Jones (Cardiff) Ltd., 41 Lochaber Street, Cardiff	£1.25
Exploring Gwynedd from Porthmadog	Showell Styles	John Jones (Cardiff) Ltd., 41 Lochaber Street, Cardiff	80p
Walking Snowdonia	Showell Styles	John Jones (Cardiff) Ltd. 41 Lochaber Street, Cardiff	50p
'Nabod Cymru	Cledwyn Fychan	Y Lolfa, Talybont, Ceredigion	45p
Walks in the Brecon Beacons	Chris Barber	Pridgeon Publishers Ltd., Marks Farmhouse, Llangrove, Ross-on-Wye, Herefordshire	76p
Exploring the Waterfall country (Ystradfellte and Pontneddfechan area)	Chris Barber	Pridgeon Publishers Ltd., Marks Farmhouse, Llangrove, Ross-on-Wye, Herefordshire	76p
Hills and Vales of the Black Mountain District	Reprint of Old Classic	Pridgeon Publishers Ltd., Marks Farmhouse, Llangrove, Ross-on-Wye, Herefordshire	£2.20
Llangollen Town and Country Walks		Alan Williams, The Lodge, Bryntysilio, Llangollen	65p
Walk in the beautiful Conwy Valley	Ralph Maddern	Focus Publications, 9 Priors Road, Windsor, Berkshire SL4 4PD	

Programmes of Guided Walks:

Brecon Beacons National Park

A programme of guided walks devised by the National Park Warden Service in co-operation with The Ramblers' Association is available from the Brecon Beacons National Park Information Centres listed in this booklet. Some of the walks are for families, arranged in conjunction with the National Museum of Wales, to areas of special interest.

The guides will turn out whatever the weather but may vary the route if conditions prove to be poor.

Forestry Commission

Talybont-on-Usk, Powys

From time to time guided walks are arranged by the Commission's staff from the Blaen-y-glyn car park (map sheet 160, reference 061171). Information is displayed in the car park some days in advance. Prior arrangements can be made for conducted tours by parties.

Gwent

An extensive programme of guided walks is available in the County of Gwent on Sundays and occasionally weekday evenings during the summer. All walks (average 3 miles in length) are lead by experienced Countryside Wardens who will point out features of interest 'en route'. The pace is leisurely with plenty of time for photography, etc.

Guides will turn out whatever the weather.

Further information from Gwent County Council, Planning Department, County Hall, Cwmbran, Gwent. Ask for the Guided Walks Programme.

Pembrokeshire Coast National Park

The Park authorities arrange each year a programme of summer guided walks in particularly interesting sections of the Park under authoritative guides who operate from the Park Information Centre located at the car park, Broad Haven, near Haverfordwest. **Details are publicised locally or can be obtained by writing to the Park Authority (address at back.)**

Penmaenmawr

Organised mountain walks with a guide are arranged by the town's Publicity Association each July and August. Details are displayed on a Notice Board at Pant-yr-afon, Penmaenmawr.

National Museum of Wales

Family Expeditions

Two series of field excursions are arranged by the National Museum of Wales annually. The 'Family Expeditions' are held in the spring and autumn when members of the staff of the Museum in Cardiff and the Welsh Folk Museum, St. Fagans, meet parents, and children in particular, in localities all over Wales where there are sites of archaeological, botanical, geological, industrial, zoological and historical interest.

The excursions are held on Saturday afternoons for some 2–3 hours, depending on weather conditions. Museum staff arrange a choice of activities at each venue. Press notices appear during the week before each expedition when members of the public are invited to apply for information regarding arrangements. **Further details may be obtained from the the Museum's Publications and Information Officer, telephone Cardiff 397951.**

Tourist Information Centres (list at back of this booklet) will have up-to-date lists of each conducted tour.

Snowdonia National Park

Snowdon Sherpa

Parking spaces in the Snowdon area are very limited but you may travel by the Snowdon Sherpa, a Circular Bus Service, from such tourist centres as Porthmadog, Beddgelert, Llanrwst, Betws-y-Coed, Capel Curig, Caernarfon and Llanberis which will take you to all the main paths leading to Snowdon and will also enable you to ascend and descend on different paths. **For Snowdon Sherpa Service leaflets write to Snowdonia National Park Information Office, Hen Ysgol, Maentwrog, Blaenau Ffestiniog, Gwynedd.**

Bus to a Walk, or Walk to a bus.

Gwynedd County Council publish a series of pamphlets which will help walkers to use buses to reach selected walks in the Snowdonia National Park. The pamphlets highlight bus services which are convenient for travelling to the starting points of various walks and also indicate return bus services from where the walk finishes.

Brief details will be given of the walks in the pamphlets, their likely duration, etc.

Pamphlets can be obtained from National Park Information Offices, local Wales Tourist Board Information Offices and Bus Operators Offices.

Youth Hostels

St. Christophers Youth Hostel

Ithon Road, Llandrindod Wells, Powys
Tel. 2474

Accommodation for Primary School and other groups with their own teachers for Educational Holidays. Up to 40 taken plus 4 leaders or staff, one group only at a time. Monday to Saturday. Individuals also taken. Door to door service and programme planned if required.

Y.H.A. Youth Hostels

The open air enthusiast finds plenty of scope in Wales for walking, rambling and climbing, and a chain of Youth Hostels is conveniently situated to enjoy the freedom of the countryside. The Youth Hostels Association has its headquarters at Trevelyan House, St. Albans, Herts. and details of membership fees may be obtained from there as well as from the following regional offices: **North Wales: 40 Hamilton Square, Birkenhead L41 5BA. (Tel. 051–647 7348/7258). South Wales: 131 Woodville Road, Cardiff CF5 4DZ. (Tel. 0222 31370).**

List of hostels in Wales:

Clwyd (*Denbighshire, Flintshire*)
Colwyn Bay; Cynwyd; Llangollen; Maeshafn, nr. Mold.

Dyfed (*Cardiganshire, Carmarthenshire, Pembrokeshire*)
Blaencaron, nr. Tregaron; Borth; Bryn Poeth Uchaf; Llanddeusant, nr. Llangadog; New Quay; Pentlepoir, nr. Tenby; Poppit Sands, nr. St. Dogmaels; Pwllderi, nr. Fishguard; St. David's; Trefin, nr. Haverfordwest; Tyncornel, nr. Llanddewi Brefi; Ystumtuen, nr. Ponterwyd.

Gwent (*Monmouthshire*)
Mounton Road, Chepstow.

Gwynedd (*Anglesey, Caernarvonshire, Merioneth*)
Bangor; Bryngwynant, Nant-gwynant; Capel Curig; Dinas Mawddwy; Ffestiniog; Idwal Cottage, Ogwen; Kings, nr. Dolgellau; Llanbedr; Llanberis; Lledr Valley; Penmaenmawr; Pen-y-Pass; Plas Rhiwaedog, nr. Bala; Ro-wen; Gerddi Bluog, Harlech.

Powys (*Breconshire, Montgomeryshire, Radnorshire*)
Capel-y-Ffin; Corris; Crickhowell; Glascwm, nr. Builth Wells; Llwyn y Celyn, Brecon; Nant-y-Dernol, Llangurig; Ty'n-y-Caeau, Brecon.

South Glamorgan
St. Athan.

West Glamorgan
Port Eynon.

Nature trails, paths and facilities

A standard format has been adopted in displaying information in this booklet, as follows:

Walk number	**1**
Nearest town or village, county	**Cemaes Bay,** Isle of Anglesey, Gwynedd
Name of trail, walk or facility with symbols showing nature of the terrain and the type of walker for whom the trail or path is primarily designed with access and parking facilities symbols	*Wylfa Nature Trail*
	P ⊖ A 1
General comments about the trail, etc.	An 8-stage trail around the seaward headland at Wylfa Head Nuclear Power Station, home of sea birds, coastal flowers and plants.
Its location	Mynydd y Wylfa. 1 mile W. of Cemaes Bay on A5025 Amlwch to Holyhead road. Map sheet 114, reference 356938.
Months of year open to visitors / Length of walk / Walking time / Charge for entry	Jan.–Dec. 1 mile 1 hour free.
Organisation from whom further information can be obtained	Central Electricity Generating Board. The Station Warden, at Gatehouse. Tel. Cemaes Bay 471
Title of publications available, and price	'Wylfa Nature Trail', 5p.
Special notes	

Unwaymarked rambles have a similar but briefer layout:

Walk number	6
Nearest town or village, / 6 figure reference of start of walk / Length of walk	Aberffraw 353688 3
	P A 1
Symbols showing: nature of the terrain; the type of walker for whom it is considered suitable; access and parking facilities	Aberffraw, 353688 W. and SW. along road to Porth Cwyfan (Church on island). Return by cliff path.
Directions, 6 figure references and bearings necessary to follow the walk	

Compass and maps are needed for most of this type of ramble

Wales
Key to Ordnance Sheet Numbers

Map 114
Anglesey

Isle of Anglesey

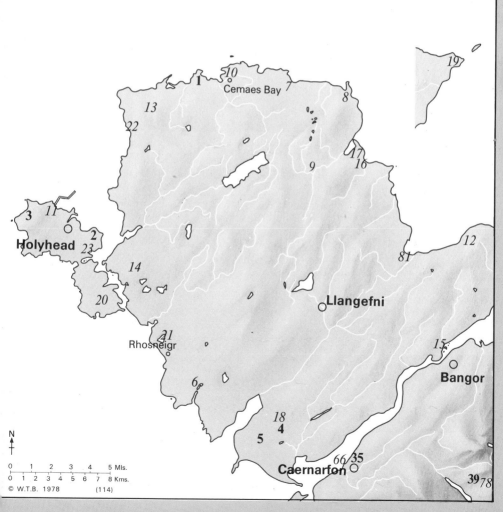

Cemaes Bay

Holyhead

Llangefni

Rhosneigr

Bangor

Caernarfon

N

| 0 | 1 | 2 | 3 | 4 | 5 Mls. |
| 0 | 1 | 2 | 3 | 4 | 5 | 6 | 7 | 8 Kms. |

© W.T.B. 1978   (114)

1

Cemaes Bay, Isle of Anglesey, Gwynedd
Wylfa Nature Trail

🅿 ⊕ A 1

An 8-stage trail around the seaward headland at Wylfa Head Nuclear Power Station, home of sea birds, coastal flowers and plants.

Mynydd y Wylfa. 1 mile W. of Cemaes Bay on A5025 Amlwch to Holyhead road. Map sheet 114, reference 356938.

Jan.–Dec. 1 mile 1 hour free.

Central Electricity Generating Board.

The Station Warden, at Gatehouse. Tel. Cemaes Bay 471

'Wylfa Nature Trail', 5p.

2

Holyhead, Isle of Anglesey, Gwynedd
Penrhos Nature Trail

🅿 ⊕ A 2

Itinerary of 13 viewing stations, illustrating rocky and sandy coast, woodlands, lakes, several historic buildings and archaeological remains.

Car and coach park at entrance to Penrhos Nature Reserve. Also picnic area, canteen and shop.

2 miles S.E. of Holyhead. Map sheet 114, reference 275804. 100 yards along road which joins A5 near Old Toll House on Stanley Embankment.

Jan.–Dec. 5 miles 4 hours free

Anglesey Aluminium Ltd., and Penrhos Nature Reserve Association.

Police Constable Ken Williams, Penrhos Nature Reserve, Holyhead Tel. 2522.

'Penrhos Nature Trail', 3p; 'Penrhos Nature Reserve', free from Warden's Office.

3

Holyhead, Isle of Anglesey, Gwynedd
South Stack Nature Trail

🅿 A 1

Nine viewing points on a guided walk down the 350 steps

South Stack lighthouse on Anglesey's north west coast, scene of the South Stack Nature Trail (item 3).

descending 150 feet to South Stack Lighthouse, with views of sea bird colonies and flowers of the coast.

3 miles W. of Holyhead. Map sheet 114, reference 206824.

May 1–mid. July 100 yds. 1hr. free.

North Wales Naturalists' Trust.

'South Stack Nature Trail', 5p.

4

Newborough, Isle of Anglesey, Gwynedd
Hendai Forest Trail

🅿 A 2 5

Hendai means 'old houses' and the trail which has 7 stations crosses the forest where tradition tells that the village of Rhosyr lies buried beneath the sand.

Llanddwyn Bay, Newborough, 14 miles S.W. of Menai Bridge off A4080 which leaves A5 at Llanfair P.G. Map sheet 114, reference 406636.

Jan.–Dec. 1 mile 40–60 mins. free

Forestry Commission

'Hendai Trail', 5p'

5

Newborough, Isle of Anglesey, Gwynedd
Newborough Warren, Ynys Llanddwyn National Nature Reserve

🅿 A 2 5

Six public access routes through 1565 acres National Nature Reserve of sandhills, salt marshes and dune grassland, substantially planted with conifers, with Ynys Llanddwyn, Cefni Estuary and Abermenai Spit.

S.W. corner of Isle of Anglesey, 12 miles from Menai Bridge on A4080 which leaves A5 at Llanfair P.G. Map sheet 114, reference 4265.

Jan.–Dec. 2–4 miles 2 hours free

Nature Conservancy, and Forestry Commission.

Leaflets (small charge) from Nature Conservancy, Penrhos Road, Bangor Tel. 4001 or Forestry Office, Newborough (Tel. 246).

6

Aberffraw	353688	3

🅿 A 1

Aberffraw, 353688 W. and SW. along road to Porth Cwyfan (Church on island). Return by cliff path.

7

Amlwch	444932	7

🅿 B 1 2

Bull Bay, Porth Wen, 427946 The whole of the coast path is good walking and can be reached from Amlwch past the school, from 430936 and from 398944.

8

Amlwch	479929	1

🅿 A 1

Porth Eilian around Point Lynas Peninsula and return.

9

Brynrefail	470850	Various

🅿 A 6

Mynydd Bodafon, 470850. There are so many paths to explore on this hill that directions are unnecessary.

10

Cemaes Bay	370935	10

🅿 ⊕ B 1

N.E. and E. by coast path E. to Dinas Brynfor (National Trust), and Porthwen, returning via Bryn Llywelyn to Cemaes.

11

Holyhead	243833	9

🅿 ⬥ ⊕ B 1

Holyhead N.W. to Soldiers' Point then W. along coast to North Stack, South Stack, S.E. to junction with main road at 218816 for return over Holyhead Mountain to Holyhead.

12

Llanddona	587813	2

🅿 A 6

Around Bwrdd Arthur Hill Fort and Old Parish Church.

13

Llanfairynghornwy	303915	2

🅿 A 1

Llanfairynghornwy 303915, path W.N.W. to Ynys-y-fydlyn, caves and cliff arch.

14

Llanfair yn Neubwll	297776	4

🅿 A 2

Llanfair yn Neubwll, from 304775, S.S.W. on minor road to airfield then S.W. to Cymyran Bay, return along beach at low tide or continue along coast to Rhosneigr.

15

Menai Bridge	554719	2

🅿 ⊕ 1 5 7

Car park near Tourist Information Centre on A5 at Coed Cyrnol, down hill through trees to Church Island on Menai Strait, E. along Strait, under Telford's Suspension Bridge to Menai Bridge and return through town.

16

Moelfre	512863	2

🅿 A 1

Moelfre N.E. to Coastguard Lookout overlooking Ynys Moelfre and return to Moelfre.

17

Moelfre	515869	3

🅿 A 2

Moelfre 515869, extension of walk from reference 512863. Continue on cliff path to Lligwy Bay (Royal Charter Monument) and return same way.

18

Newborough	424656	9

🅿 B 2 5

S.W. via forest paths to Llanddwyn Island return along sands E.S.E. 410632 to Newborough

19

Penmon	640812	2

🅿 A 1

Walks around the headland from the car parking area on the headland reached by toll gate located near Penmon Priory buildings.

20

Rhoscolyn	269759	3

🅿 A 1

W.N.W. to coast then S. to St. Gwenfaen's Well, S.E. to Coastguard Lookout and return from Borthwen to Rhoscolyn

21

Rhosneigr	319731	5

🅿 B 1 2

Rhosneigr, 319731 follow High St. to beach which follow S.S.E. to headland paths past Barclodiad y Gawres to Porth Trecastell. Follow A4048 N. to path along dunes joining A4080 S. of Llyn Maelog.

22

Rhydwyn	300892	2

🅿 A 1

Porth Swtan 300892, N. along cliffs to 296904 and back.

23

Trearddur Bay	325677	4

🅿 A 1

Trearddur Bay, 256777, S. along coast to Rhoscolyn joining walk from reference 269759, return by alternative inland paths or along coast.

Map 115
Caernarfon
and Bangor

Caernarfon and Bangor

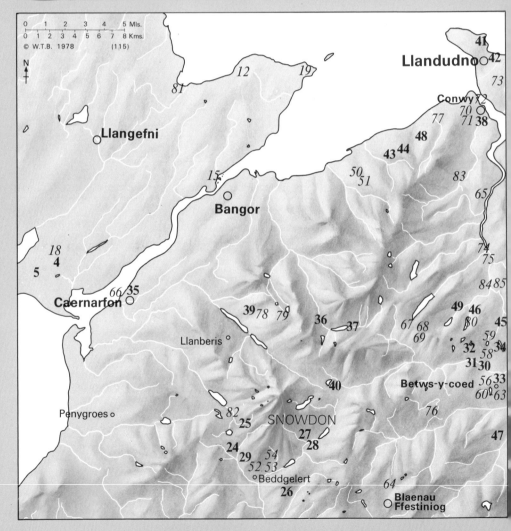

0   1   2   3   4   5 Mls.
0 1 2 3 4 5 6 7 8 Kms.
© W.T.B. 1978   (115)

N

Llandudno 41 42
73

Conwy 72
70
77   71 38

48

43 44

50
51   83

65

12   19
81

Llangefni

15

Bangor

18
4
5

66 35
Caernarfon

74
75

84 85

39 78 79   36   37   67 68   80   49 46   45
Llanberis   69   59
32 58 3
31 30

40   Betws-y-coed   56 33
60   63

82   76
25   SNOWDON   47
27
24   29   54   28
52 53
Penygroes

Beddgelert   64
26   **Blaenau
Ffestiniog**

24

Beddgelert, Gwynedd
Beddgelert Forest Trail

🅿 ⊕ A 5

Discover some of the trees of the Beddgelert Forest and its spectacular scenery on this sylvan trail.

1 mile N.W. of Beddgelert on A4085 Beddgelert – Caernarfon road. Map sheet 115, reference 578491. Start at Beddgelert Forest Camp site Car Park.

Jan.–Dec. ¾ mile 1 hour free.

Forestry Commission.
Forest Warden, Nant Colwyn (on site).

'Beddgelert Forest Trail', 5p.

Norway Spruce

25

Beddgelert, Gwynedd
Beddgelert Forest Walks, Pont Cae'r Gors

🅿 A 5 6

Beddgelert Forest lies on the west side of the A4085 Beddgelert to Caernarfon road across the slopes of the Moel Hebog range. The four waymarked walks of varying lengths explore the recesses of the forest and provide fine views across rugged scenery to nearby Snowdon.

Pont Cae'r Gors, 2½ miles north of Beddgelert on A4085. Map sheet 115, reference 575509.

Jan.–Dec. ½ mile Free.
Jan.–Dec. 1 mile Free.
Jan.–Dec. 1¾ miles Free.
Jan.–Dec. 3 miles Free.

Four walks starting from picnic place.

Forestry Commission.
Waymarked.

Guide available from 1978.

26

Beddgelert, Gwynedd
Cae Dafydd Forest Walk

🅿 A 5

A 2 mile circuit with a ¾ mile shorter route, through coniferous forest in the peaceful Nantmor Valley. Picnic site at start.

In Nantmor Valley, 3 miles S.E. of Beddgelert, off A4085 to Penrhyndeudraeth. Map sheet 115, reference 620468. Start Cae Dafydd picnic site.

Jan.–Dec. ¾ mile 1 hour free.
Jan.–Dec. 2 miles 1½ hours free.

Forestry Commission.

Walk from reference 618466 also takes in this area.

Waymarked.

27

Beddgelert, Gwynedd,
Cwm-y-Llan Nature Trail, Nant Gwynant

🅿 B 5

The walk, which follows part of the Watkin Trail leading to Snowdon Summit, demonstrates the importance for nature conservation and biological research of the Snowdon National Nature Reserves.

Bethania Bridge, 3 miles E. of Beddgelert on A 498 Beddgelert – Capel Curig road. Map sheet 115, reference 627507. Start at Hafod-y-llan farm.

Nature Conservancy.

* 2 miles 3 hours free

'Cwm-y-llan Nature Trail', (temporarily out of print for re-writing).

*Special Note: Temporarily closed due to danger from mine shaft. Expected to re-open 1978.

28

Beddgelert, Gwynedd
Nant Gwynant Walk

🅿 A 5

A short walk giving fine views of the Snowdon massif and beautiful Nant Gwynant with its lake. Steep in places.

Glanaber, Nantgwynant. Map sheet 115, reference 633512.

Jan.–Dec. ¾ mile 1hr. free.
Forestry Commission.
Waymarked only.

29

Beddgelert, Gwynedd
Wayfaring Course

🅿 ⊕ B 5

An orienteering course through mixed age conifers in Forest Main Block. Used for International Events.

Approx. ½ mile N. of Beddgelert, off A4085 at Forest campsite. Map sheet 115, reference 578491.

Jan. – Dec. Various Free.

Forestry Commission.
Detailed map and compass available at Forest office on payment of returnable deposit.

Brochure available 15p.

Sitka Spruce

30

Betws-y-Coed, Gwynedd
Garth Falls: Walk for the Handicapped and Elderly, Gwydyr Forest

🅿 ♿ ⊕ A 5

From a small car park the route passes tall spruce trees, passes close to a stream and ends with a view of a waterfall. Paved surface with seats, passing points, handrails and guide rail for blind. Suitable, with Forest Commission's exhibition, as a 'Forest Outing' for disabled.

Gwydyr Forest, Betws-y-Coed, near Miners Bridge, on south side of A5. Map 115, reference 778568.

Jan. – Dec. 300 yards various free.

Forestry Commission.

Suitable for invalid chair occupants, either self-propelled or pushed. People of limited mobility, using walking aids. The deaf and blind. The mentally retarded. Elderly people.

Groups accepted by prior arrangement with Head Forester, Llanrwst. Tel. (0492) 640578.

No brochure available.

31

Betws-y-Coed, Gwynedd
Gwydyr Forest: Cae'n-y-Coed Arboretum and Walk

P A 5

There are two walks, the longer is steep in places and climbs through the Arboretum providing fine views of Snowdon and the Llugwy Valley. A short, easy walk is suitable for the less agile.

The Arboretum contains 48 tree species, numbered for identification from a guide.

On the A5 between Betws-y-Coed and Capel Curig, Map sheet 115, reference 763572.

1. Jan.–Dec. ¾ ml. 40–60 mins. free.
2. Jan.–Dec. 300 yds. 10–15 mins. free.

Forestry Commission

Gwydyr Uchaf, Llanrwst. Tel. 640578.

'Cae'n-y-Coed Arboretum and Walk', 5p.

32

Betws-y-Coed, Gwynedd
Gwydyr Forest Trail

P B 5

Thirteen stages illustrate the work of the forester in his task of re-afforestation in an area of great natural beauty.

On the north bank of Llugwy from Ty Hyll (Ugly House) to Miners Bridge, Betws-y-Coed on A5. Map sheet 115, reference 759578.

Jan.–Dec. 3 miles 3 hours free.

Forestry Commission.

'Gwydyr Forest Trail', 10p.

33

Betws-y-Coed, Gwynedd
Short Walks in Betws-y-Coed area

P A 6

Nine short walks through woods, over hills and along public footpaths, all suitable for family strolls.

Betws-y-Coed, Gwynedd. Map sheet 115.

Jan.–Dec. free.

Name	Miles	Hrs.
1. *Miners Bridge and River Walk*	¾	1
2. *Park Lake (Llyn-y-Parc) and Cyrau View*	2¾	2
3. *The Quarry and Garth Eryr Loop*	2½	2
4. *Jubilee Path and Fire Lookout*	2½	3
5. *Lledr Panorama*	1¼	1½
6. *Llannerch Elsi Loop*	2¾	3
7. *Fairy Glen and Conwy Falls*	2	1½
8. *Rhiwddolion and Pont-y-pant*	4	3
9. *Suspension Bridge*	1	1

Simple duplicated sheet, price 2p, available from the Tourist Information Centre, Betws-y-Coed.

34

Betws-y-Coed, Gwynedd
Ten Walks in the Gwydyr Forest

P A 5

Gwydyr Forest lies on the A5 London to Holyhead road in Snowdonia National Park and forms the back-ground for the attractive village of Betws-y-Coed. The ten routes explore places in the forest and reveal some breathtaking views.

Gwydyr Forest, Start at Pont-y-pair, Betws-y-Coed. Map sheet 115, reference 790568.

Jan.–Dec. free.

Name	Miles	Hrs.
Church Walk	¾	½
Cyrau Walk	2	1
Llugwy Gorge	4½ / 2½	2½ / 1½
Plateau Walk	4	2½
Drws Gwyn	3	2½
Llyn Sarnau	5¼	3½
Craig Forys	1¾	1
Llyn Glangors	2¼	1¼
Artist's Wood	1½	1¼
Chapel Walk	¾	½

Forestry Commission.

'Ten Walks in Gwydyr Forest', 20p.

35

Caernarfon, Gwynedd
Caernarfon Town Trail

P A 7

Short walk in the historic walled town of Caernarfon.

Caernarfon, map sheet 115.

Jan.–Dec. ¾ mile 30 mins. free.

Caernarfon Borough Council, Caernarfon.

'Caernarfon Town Trail' illustrated, 3p.

36

Capel Curig, Gwynedd
Cwm Idwal Nature Trail

P B 6

The trail of 11 stations illustrates past glaciation, rocks and soils and the plants and animals of the Cwm Idwal National Nature Reserve.

Llyn Idwal, near Ogwen Cottage Mountain School, 4½ miles W. of Capel Curig on A5 Capel Curig to Bethesda road. Map sheet 115, reference 648603.

Jan.–Dec. 2 miles 3 hours free

Nature Conservancy.

Cwm Idwal National Nature Reserve: Nature Trail, 5p (10p plus s.a.e. by post).

37

Capel Curig, Gwynedd
Gwern-y-gof Uchaf Farm Trail

P A 4

In open mountain, with a climb of some 200 feet, the walk demonstrates the working of a hill farm in rough country.

3 miles W. of Capel Curig on A5 Capel Curig to Bethesda road. Map sheet 115, reference 673604. Jan.–Dec. 1 mile 1 hour free

Snowdonia National Park Authority with farm's operator.

Information boards along route.

Conwy, Gwynedd
Conwy Town Trail

P ⊟ ⊕ A 7

A walk around interesting sites in ancient walled and castled Conwy including: Porth Bach, the Fish Quay, Lower Gate (Porth Isaf), the smallest house in Great Britain, Porth yr Aden (Wing Gate), the Town Wall Walk, Wall Walk, Telford's Arch, Porth Uchaf (Upper Gate), Llywelyn's Tower, the Conwy Cockpit, Plas Mawr, Aberconwy House, Black Lion House, St. Mary's Church, Exchequer Castle, Telford's Suspension Bridge, Stephenson's Tubular Bridge.

Conwy on A55 North Wales coast road. Map sheet 115, reference 783777.

Jan.–Dec. 1¾ miles 1 hour free.*

North Wales Tourism Council, Conwy Civic Society, Aberconwy District Council, and other bodies.

Descriptive leaflet, 'Conwy Town Trail', small charge, available at Information Centre.

*Charge: Entrance fees to Wall Walk, smallest house, Plas Mawr, Aberconwy House, Conwy Castle.

Llanberis, Gwynedd
Llyn Padarn Country Park, Walks and Trails

P ⊕ 5 6 7

Llyn Padarn Country Park, beside the lake, locked between the mountains of the Moel Eilio and Elidir Fawr, was formed from Dinorwic Slate Quarry and the Allt Wen woodlands of the Faynol Estate. Its outstanding building is now the North Wales Quarrying Museum and the former quarry rail line is now Llanberis Lake Railway.

Llanberis, on A4086 Caernarfon to Capel Curig road. Map sheet 115, reference 586603.

There is a series of three walks:

Allt Wen Woodland Nature Trail
Jan.–Dec. ½ mile 1 hour free.

Vivian Quarry Trail
Jan.–Dec. ¼ mile ¾ hour free.

Woodland Walks (to 14 places of interest)

Jan.–Dec.   various   free.
Gwynedd County Council.
Brochures available on site.

40

Llanberis, Gwynedd
The Miners Track, Pen-y-pass

P ⊕ B 6

The described route of 2 miles from Pen-y-pass Youth Hostel towards Llyn Llydaw leads on to Snowdon summit.

Pen-y-pass Youth Hostel, 5 miles S.E. of Llanberis on A4086. Caernarfon to Capel Curig road. Map sheet 115, reference 648558.

Jan.–Dec. 2 miles 3 hours free.

Nature Conservancy.

'Snowdon National Nature Reserve – The Miners Track' 5p.

Llandudno, Gwynedd
Great Orme Nature Trail

P ⊟ ⊕ A 1

A trail of 18 viewing stations from Happy Valley by way of woodland and heath, cliff and shore, bare rock and cultivated land back to exotic Haulfre Gardens, with superb views of the resort and Conwy Bay to Snowdonia.

Llandudno, Happy Valley, near the Pier, Map sheet 115, reference 782832.

Jan.–Dec. 5 miles 3 hours free.

Aberconwy District Council, Llandudno and North Wales Naturalists' Trust.

'Llandudno Great Orme Nature Trail', 4p.

Great Orme Nature Trail
The 5 miles trail starts by the Cafe in Happy Valley. Suitable points for breaking your journey would be: station 4 to return via Wyddfyd; 6 and 7 to catch the tramway for town or summit (station 9) where you have a choice of tram or cable.

Station	Point of interest
1.	Glacial valley. Gorsedd stones.
2.	Happy Valley Rock Gardens.
3.	Mountain hawthorn and Wyddfyd.
4.	View towards Pen-y-dinas hill fort.
5.	Pen-y-mynydd Isaf farm.
6.	Conwy views. Divert for cromlech.
7.	2,000 years old copper mine shafts.
8.	Coral fossils in Bishop's Quarry.
9.	Great Orme summit – extensive views.
10.	Long hut marks, St. Tudno's church.
11.	Hafnant Valley – flowers.
12.	The limestone pavement.
13.	Marine Drive – ancient dwellings.
14.	Views of Anglesey and Puffin Island.
15.	Gogarth Abbey remains, butterflies.
16.	Alice in Wonderland memorials.
17.	Haulfre Gardens – rare trees.
18.	End of the trail.

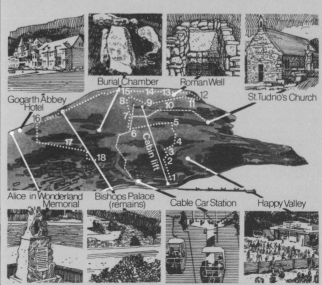

42

Llandudno, Gwynedd
Llandudno Town Trail

P ⇄ ⊛ A 7

A short walk around the town's attractive hotel and residential area at the foot of the Great Orme. The architecture and planning illustrates well how Llandudno developed as a seaside resort under the Mostyn Estates.

Llandudno, Map sheet 115, reference 783827. Start at Cenotaph on promenade.

Jan.–Dec. 2 miles 1½–2 hrs. free.

Llandudno Civic Society and Aberconwy District Council, Llandudno.

'Llandudno Town Trail', 10p.

43

Llanfairfechan, Gwynedd
Coedydd Aber Nature Trail

P B 5

A scenic walk through natural woodlands to the spectacular Aber Falls on Rhaeadr-fawr.

Bontnewydd, ½ mile S.E. of Aber Village which lies 2 miles S.W. of Llanfairfechan on A55 Conwy – Bangor road. Map sheet 115, reference 662720.

Jan.–Dec. 3 miles 3 hours free.

Nature Conservancy.

'Coedydd Aber Nature Trail', 10p.

44

Llanfairfechan, Gwynedd
Llanfairfechan History Trail

P ⇄ ⊛ B 6 7

A historic tour of a hilly area taking in a Roman road, hut circles, standing stones and panoramic views of the North Wales coast and mountains.

Llanfairfechan, Valley road leading to Bwlch-y-Ddeufaen. Start: Three streams car park and picnic site, Valley road, 1 mile S.E. of Llanfairfechan. Map sheet 115, reference 698736.

Jan.–Dec. 4½ ml. 2½–3½ hrs. free.

Llanfairfechan Amenities Association.

'Llanfairfechan History Trail', available locally.

45

Llanrwst, Gwynedd
Lady Mary's Walk, Gwydyr Forest

P ⇄ ⊛ A 5

A short undemanding walk with 7 stops introducing the work of the Forestry Commission.

Gwydyr Uchaf, a mansion – now offices – at Llanrwst on B5106, Conwy to Betws-y-Coed road. Map sheet 115, reference 796608.

Jan.–Dec. 1 ml. 40–60 mins. free.

Forestry Commission.

'Lady Mary's Walk', 5p.

46

Llanrwst, Gwynedd
Llyn Geirionydd Forest Trail (See also Walk No. 80

P A 5

Three-quarter mile walk showing various aspects of forestry and lead mining, which once flourished here in the heart of the mountains.

Llyn Geirionnydd 3 miles W. of Llanrwst on B5106 Conwy – Betws-y-Coed road.

Map Sheet 115, reference 762604.

Jan.–Dec. ¾ ml. 40–60 mins. free.

Forestry Commission.

'Llyn Geirionnydd Trail', 5p.

47

Penmachno, Gwynedd
Penmachno Wayfaring Course

P B 5 6

The Competitive sport of orienteering – in its introductory form, wayfaring – finds an outlet here in spectacular mountain and wooded scenery on the slopes above the beautiful Machno.

Maps available at Penmachno Post Office, on B4406, Betws-y-Coed – Ffestiniog road. Map sheet 115, reference 789504.

Jan.–Dec. Various – free.

Forestry Commission.

Brochure available, 15p.

48

Penmaenmawr, Gwynedd
Penmaenmawr History Trail

P ⇄ ⊛ B 6 7

A walk on the 1500 ft high hills behind the town to places of interest dating from the Bronze and Iron Ages through to mediaeval times, with magnificent sea views.

Penmaenmawr on A55, 5 miles W. of Conwy. Map sheet 115, reference 720759, Graiglwyd Farm

Jan.–Dec. 3½ miles 2–3 hours free

Penmaenmawr Historical Society.

'History Trail on the uplands of Penmaenmawr' 5p, available locally.

49

Trefriw, Gwynedd
Crafnant Walk

P A 3 5

The tiny mountain-ringed reservoir of Crafnant, high in the hills south-west of Trefriw, is the setting for a walk in an idyllic wooded situation, with viewpoint.

Llyn Crafnant, 1½ mile S.W. of Trefriw, reached by side road off B5106 Llanrwst to Dolgarrog road. Map sheet 115, reference 754616. Start at N.W. point of the reservoir.

Jan.–Dec. ¾ ml. 1 hour free

Forestry Commission.
Waymarked only.

50

Aber   653726

P B 5 6

S. to Aber Falls, S.W. to 650690 the pass between Moel Wnion and Gyrn to 640697 for path N.E. to Aber.

51

Aber   663720   6 or 10

P B 5

From 663720 cross bridge and up track, then N.E. to 675720 and S. and S.E. to Llyn Anafon and back, or drop to Llanfairfechan from 675720 for coast path to Aber.

52

| Beddgelert | 590481 | 4 |

P B 5

Tough – not for misty weather

From village go S.W. to Cwm Cloch and Moel Hebog N.W. and W. to near Ogof Owen Glyndwr then down Cwm Meillionen and back via Cwm Cloch.

53

| Beddgelert | 590481 | 8 |

P B 5

To Llyn Dinas, keeping S. of Afon Glaslyn, and Hafod Owen, Blaen Nantmor, Nantmor and back through Aberglaslyn Pass.

54

| Beddgelert | 604490 | 4 |

P A 5

Past Dinas Emrys for road around N.W. side of Llyn Dinas to bridge beyond Bryn Dinas for return from Bethania by roads and path along S. side to Llyn Dinas.

55

| Betws-y-Coed | 779568 | 4 |

P ⊞ ⊕ A 5 6

Rhiwddolion to Pont-y-Pant. Take the Capel Curig road as far as the Miner's Bridge. Opposite the bridge take the path to the left and left again where the path divides. This route leads to the upland hamlet of Rhiwddolion. Here the road is rather steep. The road leads down through forest and hill scenery to come out on the A470 at Pont-y-Pant. From here walk or take the train back to Betws-y-Coed.

56

| Betws-y-Coed | 781538 | 2¾ |

P ⊞ ⊕ A 5 6

Llanerch Elsi Loop. Starts at Gethin's Bridge stone viaduct crossing A470 approximately 2 miles from the village. The footpath begins 50 yards up a private road immediately behind the bridge, rising sharply through dense pine woods to Llanerch Elsi and along to Lake Elsi. Return by

crossing the plateau to Giants Head (791541) and down to A470 road.

57

| Betws-y-Coed | 792568 | 2¾ |

P ⊞ ⊕ 5 6

Llyn y Parc and Clogwyn, start from Pont-y-Pair car park, turn right between Summerhill and From Heulog. After about 200 yards you come to a signpost marked Cyrau and Park Lake. Take Cyrau sign, steep path through the woods to a stile at the top. After leaving the wood the the path bends gradually round the hill through heather moorlands to the summit. From here there are excellent views. Walk back to the junction of 'Coloured' paths and take route through the woods. Llyn y Parc is reached on even ground. Leave the lake on the return journey by a path that descends through a narrow ravine. The path leads past the old Aberllyn lead mine, through the wood and back to the car park. (For alternative walk to Llyn y Parc see walk from reference 794565.)

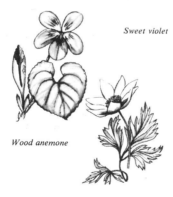

Sweet violet

Wood anemone

58

| Betws-y-Coed | 792568 | ¾ |

P ⊞ ⊕ A 5

Miner's Bridge and River Walk. From Pont-y-Pair Bridge turn left through the car park and follow the river bank path to the Miner's Bridge. Cross the bridge, taking care if wet, and return to Betws-y-Coed down the main road (A5).

59

| Betws-y-Coed | 794565 | 6 |

P ⊞ ⊕ B 5 6

N. to Llyn y Parc, 783587, W. and S. to Diosgydd and footpath via Miners Bridge. See walk from reference 792568.

60

| Betws-y-Coed | 794565 | 2 or 7 |

P ⊞ ⊕ A/B 5 6

From church to Llyn Elsi, Rhiw Goch, Hafod Las and back (or direct Llyn Elsi to Hafod Las for short route).

61

| Betws-y-Coed | 794565 | 6 |

P ⊞ ⊕ B 5 6

Betws-y-Coed E. via Waterloo Bridge to Capel Garmon, S. to Burial Chamber at 818543, S. then S.W. A5, cross to Conwy Falls – Beaver Bridge and return to Betws-y-Coed by side roads. (See also walk 816555 on sheet 116.)

62

| Betws-y-Coed | 797542 | 2 |

P ⊞ ⊕ A 5 6

Fairy Glen and Conwy Falls. Start at the Beaver Bridge, road through this gateway to Fairy Glen (on sheet 116) and Conwy Falls. Follow Pentrefoelas road for ½ mile past Pandy Mill and Roman Bridge. Follow left bank of the Conwy through a wood to the Lledr Bridge. Turn right back to the Beaver Bridge following either bank of the river.

63

| Betws-y-Coed | 799538 | 5 |

P ⊞ ⊕ A 5

S.W. to Ty Mawr (see reference in walk from reference 736525). Return through Cyfyng and track by River Lledr.

64

| Blaenau Ffestiniog | 702488 | 9 |

P ⊞ ⊕ B 6

Crimea Pass, W. and N.W. round N. side of Moel Dyrnogydd

to Lledr Valley headwaters around Nhadog Isaf, E.N.E. to junction with A470 near Roman Bridge at 716513 via Gorddinan or Blaenau Dolwyddelan, for return via same route (to avoid traffic on busy A470) to start.

65

Caerhun	773704	5

P ⊕ **A 6**

From 773704 (hourly bus, restricted parking at church) lane E to Caerhun Church and Canovium Roman Fort, N.N.E. to B5279. Follow this W. to path to 776724 and then path to Glyn Uchaf. Return by lanes and path to start.

66

Caernarfon	478627	6

P ⇆ **B 2 4**

W. over Seiont Bridge at Caernarfon, past Swimming Bath to old Church at 454607, W. and N.W. to Plas Farm and back to start at Caernarfon.

67

Capel Curig	722582	10

P B 6

N. on A5 from village to Bron Heulog then to Llyn Cowlyd dam, S.E. to Lledwigan S.W. via Llyn Crafnant to Cornel Farm, S.W. and W. to start.

68

Capel Curig	722582	5

P B 6

Follow previous walk to south end of Llyn Cowlyd at 717609. Then take path W., S.S.W. to Tal-y-braich at 692602. Cross A5 main road and stream to join old road back to Capel Curig.

69

Capel Curig	731576	3

P A 6

Cobdens Hotel W. over the Afon Llugwy to woodland footpath W. to Brynengan at 716577 cross to Mountain Rescue Post, to Post Office for return on track E. to 732582, thence F.P. to school and Cobdens Hotel.

Curlew

Hare-Bell

Scots Pine

Hare

Carrion Crow

Long-tailed Field Mouse

Bracken

Hare-Bell

WTB © 1978

Hillsides, moorland, heath and mountains.

Buzzard

Buzzard

Stonechat

70

Conwy	749770	7

P B 6 7

From Sychnant Pass S. to 740750, W. to Stone Circle, back via Bryn Derwydd and Capelulo. Can be taken from Penmaenmawr (see Penmaenmawr History Trail).

71

Conwy	749770	3–4

P A 6

From Sychnant Pass N. to Conwy Mountain for various tracks to Conwy or back to starting point.

72

Conwy	769759	6 or 10

P ⇌ ⊕ B 6

From Conwy take road to Groesffordd 769759 (or park there). Up to Llechwedd Old Church, 751738. Path S. then paths through fields to Rowen. Drop to B5106 for hourly bus (6 m) or take path to Rhiw 746721, then N. and N.W. to standing stone, 739736 from where there are tracks to Conwy.

73

Deganwy	783789	8

P ⇌ B 4

Starts and finishes on sheet 115 but substantially on sheet 116. Deganwy Church to Castle, N.E. to Llanrhos, Bryn Maelgwyn woods, E. to 808812, track S.E. past Gloddaeth Isaf to Glanwydden, S.W. along path to Pydew at 812795, through Bodysgallen grounds, paths back to Deganwy.

74

Dolgarrog	732663	4

P ⊕ 5 6

From 732663 (some parking) track to Melynllyn, Dulyn, 718675 and back.

75

Dolgarrog	769678	3½

P ⊕ 5 6

From 769678, Dolgarrog (hourly bus, some parking), lane W. becoming a path, then stile to S. to Porth Llwyd Falls 764675. Continue up stream to road which follow to 758668 at leat which follow N.E. and E. to 764670, then down old rail track to a junction of pipes. Take stiles on R (765672) to zig-zag path through woods to start.

76

Dolwyddelan	736525	6

P ⇌ B 5 6

From church go S. past station, E. over mountain to Ty Mawr, where Bishop Morgan (1545–1604) first translator of Bible into Welsh, lived. (National Trust). Go S. along road to 775510 returning W.N.W. via Pigyn Esgob and Bwlch-y-groes to Pentre Bont.

77

Dwygyfylchi nr. Penmaen- mawr	731759	2

P A 6

Jubilee Walk S.E. from village of Dwygyfylchi for a circuit around the peak of Foel Lus.

78

Llanberis	583597	4

P A 6

W. side of Afon Arddu to waterfall then to Ceunant for return down lane past Youth Hostel to Llanberis.

79

Llanberis	586603	4–6

P ⊕ A 5 6

Country Park near terminus of Llanberis Lake Railway Station, zigzags N. to Hafodty, then N. to Dinorwic and W. along road to Fachwen for return by woodland path to Country Park.

80

Llanrwst	764604	3

P A 5 6

From picnic site around Llyn Geirionnydd and back.

81

Pentraeth	524784	6

P B 2 6

Pentraeth, 524784, follow B5109 to 535783 and Forestry Commission road over Mynydd Llwydiarth with possible diversion at 547790 to lake and back, to 558798. N.W. to Ty-mawr and beach which follow to 532798 for path past Fron Goch to start.

82

Rhyd-Ddu	572526	6

P B 6

Rhyd-Ddu car park W. and S.W. by footpath under Mynydd Drws-y-Coed to Parc Cae-cra at 556510, E. via Parc Cae-mawr to Pont Cae'r Gors and return to start along old railway.

83

Rowen	758720	5

P ⊕ A 6

From Rowen 758720 (2 hourly bus and parking), follow street, turn N.W. at 756720 past Rhiw to Cae Coch noting Roman field system on N. and S. Either walk to Bwlch-y-Ddeufaen and return, or drop straight to Roman Bridge at 739708. Return by road to Rowen at 738710.

84

Trefriw	780631	4½

P ⊕ B 6

Trefriw 780631 (hourly bus and parking), follow road to Llyn Crafnant, return to 757618, track and path E. to monument at Llyn Geirionydd. Road to Llanrychwyn Old Church 774617 and back to start.

85

Trefriw	780631	6

P ⊕ B 6

From Trefriw 780631 (hourly bus, parking) take Crafnant road, branch right to Cowlyd Road, branch at 773639 to Rhibo, 773651, path W. to road at 765653, then S.W. to Llyn Cowlyd. Return to 743642 and take track by Brwynog to start.

Map 116
Denbigh and
Colwyn Bay

Denbigh and Colwyn Bay

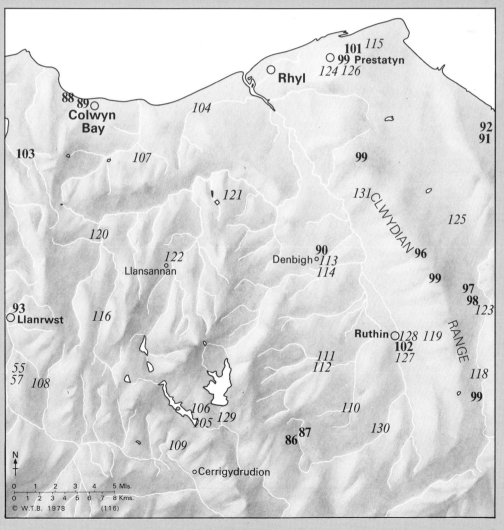

101 *115*
○ **99** Prestatyn
124 126
○ Rhyl

88 89○
Colwyn
Bay

104

92
91

103

107

99

121

131 CLWYDIAN

125

120

122
○
Llansannan

90
Denbigh○*113*
114

96

99

97
98
123

93
○Llanrwst

116

Ruthin○*128 119*
102
127

RANGE

55
57 *108*

111
112

118

99

106
105 *129*

110

130

N

109

86 87

○Cerrigydrudion

0   1   2   3   4   5 Mls.
0 1 2 3 4 5 6 7 8 Kms.
© W.T.B. 1978   (116)

21

86/87

Clocaenog, Clwyd
Bod Petrual Visitor Centre

P A 5

An exhibition presenting the forest in its ecological, and historical setting in the locality is displayed in an old keeper's cottage situated in a forest clearing above a small lake, beautifully set among old larch, pine and broadleaved trees. Bod Petrual Picnic Place. Picnic tables are set under pine trees and in an open grassy place by the lake. Toilets. (Suitable for Wheelchairs.)

Pont Petryal, 7 miles S.W. of Ruthin by B5105. Map sheet 116, reference 036511. Start from visitor centre.

Jan.–Dec. Various, ½ hour free. ¼ mile to 3 to hours 2¾ miles

Forestry Commission.

Bod Petrual Walks. Waymarked walks from ¼ m to 2¾m through woodlands of many species around the lake and with a glimpse of the moors beyond.

Guide 10p from dispenser at information board.

88

Colwyn Bay, Clwyd
Bryn Euryn Nature Trail

P A 6

Scenic nature trail with points of historic interest, natural beauty spots, marked viewpoint at top of hill, wonderful views of the coast and Snowdonia. Area designated as a site of special scientific interest – because of its flora and fauna.

Between Rhos on Sea and Mochdre. Map sheet 116, reference 834798.

Jan.–Dec. 1–1½ mls. 1–1½ hrs. free.

North Wales Naturalists' Trust in conjunction with Colwyn District Council.

'Bryn Euryn Nature Trail', small charge, available at Prince of Wales Information Centre.

Visitors to the area who might wish to see more exotic fauna should visit Colwyn Bay's Mountain Zoo about 1 mile SE of Bryn Euryn.

89

Colwyn Bay, Clwyd
Colwyn Bay Town Trail

P ⬛ ⊕ A 7

The resort of Colwyn Bay has grown since 1865 around a sandy bay overlooked by wooded heights. This brochure takes the visitor on a journey into the town's past.

Colwyn Bay on A55. Map sheet 116. Reference 8578.

Jan.–Dec. 2 miles 1½ hours free.

Colwyn Bay Civic Society.

Brochure, 10p. Available locally.

90

Denbigh, Clwyd
Denbigh Town Trail

P ⊕ A 7

Established as part of European Architectural Heritage Year, 1975, this trail takes you through a town steeped in history. Buildings date from Mediaeval, Georgian and Regency periods.

Denbigh, Vale of Clwyd, at junction of A525 with A543, Map sheet 116, reference 0566.

Jan.–Dec. 1½ miles ¾ hour free.

Clwyd County Council.

'Denbigh Town Trail', 12p.

91

Holywell, Clwyd
Holywell Nature Trail

P ⊕ A 5 7

Trail covers a wooded river valley, 12th century Basingwerk Abbey, and the ancient holy well from which the town takes its name.

Pen-y-Maes Estate, near Holywell High School, off A5026 Flint – Holywell road, Map sheet 116, reference 195764.

Start: A side road bounding Pen-y-maes estate on its east side.

Jan.–Dec. 3 miles 3 hours free.

Clwyd County Council and local schools.

'Holywell Nature Trail', 12p. Ancient Monuments leaflet on Basingwerk Abbey, small charge, from H.M.S.O.

92

Holywell, Clwyd
Holywell Town Trail

P ⬛ ⊕ A 7

An illustrated walk around an interesting old town whose main feature is St. Winifred's Well and adjoining Chapel believed erected for Lady Mary Beaufort, mother of King Henry VII.

Holywell, between Flint and Prestatyn on A548 coast road. Map sheet 116.

Jan.–Dec. 1 mile 1 hour free.

Clwyd County Council.

'Holywell Town Trail', 5p.

For further information on footpaths in the Holywell – Stokyn – Greenfield and Holywell – Pantasaph – Pen-y-ball areas ask for leaflets Nos. 1 and 2 respectively from Delyn District Council, Dept. of Technical Services, Guildhall, Flint. Tel. 3551.

93

Llanrwst, Gwynedd
Llanrwst and District Trail

P ⬛ ⊕ A 7

A tour around the ancient buildings of the historic town of Llanrwst starting at the shapely 17th century arched bridge, in an area of great scenic beauty.

Llanrwst, on A470, Map sheet 116, reference 798616, 3 miles north of Betws-y-Coed.

Jan.–Dec. 2 miles 1½ hours free. (around town)

Dyffryn Conwy Civic Society.

'Llanrwst and District Trail', 5p, available locally.

94

Mold, Clwyd
Loggerheads Country Park

P A 5

A woodland park in the valley of the River Alyn with views, information centre and nature trail.

2 miles west of Mold on A494. Map sheet 116, reference 198629.

Jan.–Dec. Various walks   free.
and
Nature Trail
Clwyd County Council and
Countryside Commission.

95

Mold, Clwyd
Loggerheads Nature Trail

 P ⊕ A 5

A 12-stage walk from Loggerheads Inn along the River Alyn
and the leat that worked old mill
wheels through a limestone area
with associated plants, flowers,
animals and birds.
3 miles W. of Mold at Loggerheads Inn on A494 Mold –
Ruthin road. Map sheet 116,
reference 198626.
Jan.–Dec. 1¼ miles 2 hours free.
Clwyd County Council and
local schools.
'Loggerheads Nature Trail', 5p.

96

Mold, Clwyd
Moel Arthur Country Park

P A 6

A moorland country park in the
Clwydian Hills which has within
its boundaries a hill fort, Offa's
Dyke Path and fine views of the
Vale of Clwyd.
Moel Arthur, 5 miles distant
from Mold, Ruthin, Denbigh and
Holywell. Map sheet 116,
reference 1466.
Jan.–Dec. Various walks,   free.
Offa's Dyke Path
and Nature Trail
Clwyd County Council and
Countryside Commission.

97

Mold, Clwyd
Moel Fammau Country Park

P A 6

A moorland park in the southern
area of the Clwydian Range. It
has fine views, a reservoir, Jubilee
Tower, a hill fort and Offa's
Dyke Path.
Moel Fammau 6 miles S.W. of
Mold. Map sheet 116, reference
1662.

Jan.–Dec. Various walks   free.
and Offa's Dyke
Path
Clwyd County Council and
Countryside Commission.

98

Mold, Clwyd
Moel Fammau Nature Trail

P ⊕ A 6

Twelve viewing stations through
Clwyd Forest to Moel Fammau
summit. It has trees, plants and

99/100
Offa's Dyke path

Prestatyn, (Clwyd) to
Chepstow, (Gwent)

P ⇄ ⊕ A B C 4 5 6 7

Built in the 8th century by King
Offa of Mercia, this 167 miles
dyke walk runs the length of
the Wales – England border
closely following the present day
boundary. The dyke defended
Offa's England from marauding

birds, Bronze Age cairns and
views over the Vale of Clwyd.
At Coed Clwyd, 5 miles W. of
Mold on a side road leaving
A494 Mold – Ruthin road at
Tafarn-y-gelyn or Llanferres. Map
sheet 116, reference 174612.
Jan.–Dec. 2–4 miles 3 hours free.
Clwyd and Liverpool Education
Committee and Forestry
Commission.
'Moel Fammau Nature Trail',
5p. (See also walks from references
116/161605 and 161/126585 for
alternative routes to Moel
Fammau).

Welsh and has ever since been
looked upon as the symbolic
dividing line between the two
nations.
Crossing and recrossing the
present Wales/England border
from north to south. Covered by
map sheets 116, 117, 126, 137,
148, 161, 162.
Jan.–Dec. 167 miles 3 weeks free.
Countryside Commission.

List of main publications:

	Author	Published by	Price
Offa's Dyke	Arthur Roberts	Ramblers Association	15p
The O.D.A. Book of Offa's Dyke,	Frank Noble	Offa's Dyke Association, Old Primary School,	£1.40
2nd edition, revised		West Street, Knighton, Powys and Thornhill Press, Gloucester	
Through Welsh Border Country following Offa's Dyke Path	Mark Richards	Thornhill Press Ltd., 46 Westgate Street, Gloucester	£1.95
Offa's Dyke Path	John B. Jones	Her Majesty's Stationery Office (for the Country-side Commission)	£2.50
Strip maps at 1 in. and 2 in. scales for complete Offa's Dyke Path (9 double-sided sheets in polythene packet)	O.D.A.	Offa's Dyke Association, Old Primary School, West Street, Knighton, Powys	£1.40
Offa's Dyke Path, Prestatyn to Oswestry		Clwyd County Council	5p

A complete list of publications available on the Offa's Dyke Path
and environs can be obtained from the Offa's Dyke Association, Old
Primary School, West Street, Knighton, Powys LD7 1EW by sending
a stamped, addressed foolscap envelope.

101

Prestatyn, Clwyd
Bishopswood Nature Trail

P ⇌ ⊕ A 5

Twelve viewing stations in a woodland setting with panoramic views over North Wales to Great Orme, Llandudno, Anglesey and Snowdon.

Above St. Melyd Golf Course, Meliden, on S. side of Prestatyn. Map sheet 116, reference 068813. Approximately 10 minutes' walk from the centre of Prestatyn. (See also walk from reference 065803 on Map sheet 116.)

Jan.–Dec. 2 miles 1 hour free.

Rhuddlan Borough Council.

'Bishopswood Nature Trail', 3p.

102

Ruthin, Clwyd
A walk around historic Ruthin

P A 7

Mediaeval, Georgian, Regency and Victorian buildings make Ruthin, in the Vale of Clwyd, one of the most visually appealing historic towns in Wales.

Distinctive half-timbered black and white architecture, so much a feature of Ruthin and district.

In Ruthin, Map sheet 116, reference 125584. Start in Cae Ddol car park near river bridge at Denbigh entrance to town; at Dog Lane near Wynnstay Arms and Plas Coch, or at Station Yard, Park Road.

Jan.–Dec. 3 walks each free.
1 mile, of 1 hour

Clwyd County Council.

'A walk around historic Ruthin', small charge.

103

Talycafn, Gwynedd
Walks in Bodnant Garden

P ⊕ A 4

One of Britain's best gardens, given to the State by Lord Aberconway in 1949. It has fine early summer displays of rhododendrons and azaleas as well as magnificent summer border displays, flowering trees and shrubs.

Bodnant Garden in the Vale of Conwy, given to the State in 1949 by Lord Aberconwy, is open for public visits.

On A470 8 miles S. of Llandudno Junction. Map sheet 116, reference 802722.

*Spring to Various Entrance fee
autumn walks

National Trust.

'The Garden of Bodnant'.

*Opening times and entrance charges change from time to time. The most up-to-date position should be obtained by ringing your nearest Tourist Information Centre (see back of book).

104

Abergele	944776	5

P ⇌ ⊕ B 4 6

From Abergele path (starting through estate) then lane to Tyddyn Uchaf (932763), paths to 917765 and round S. cliffs of Pen-y-corddyn Mawr; cross river N. to Bryn Dulas, then take path S. along cliff to Pentre Du (901767); lane and paths to Llysfaen (888772), and path to Penmaenrhôs. Return by bus.

105

Alwen Reservoir	953537	3½

P A 3 5

From picnic site car park, walk W. along water edge N. side of reservoir for 1½ miles. At end of forestry plantation turn right, follow stream for ¼ mile and then right again on to forest ride and back to starting point.

106

Alwen Reservoir	955530	4½

P A 3 5 6

From car park at base of dam, cross dam and follow edge of reservoir for ¼ mile. Turn left at stream and follow uphill (across main forest ride) to edge of forestry plantation. Follow edge of plantation uphill to farm buildings and continue along F.P. around edge of forest, to Craig-yr-iyrchen summit. Continue round to next forest ride, turn right and go straight downhill to reservoir thence turn right along edge back to starting point.

107

Betws-yn-Rhos	907736	4½

P ⊕ A 4 6

From village centre take Colwyn Road, turn left by Farm Hotel and 200 yards. Left again on second track and F.P. near

Nant-y-Fedw. After ¾ mile uphill, turn right on lane to Pant-y-Clyd. Go W. through gate on F.P., downhill and on to path following river valley. Right at first farm (Bron Pistyll), on track leading to road back into village.

108

Capel Garmon, nr.   **816555**   **5**
Llanrwst

🅿   A   5   6

Road S.E. then path to Burial Chamber, Penrhyddian, bridleway N.W. past Graeanllyn to start.

109

Cefn brith   **932506**   **8**

🅿   B   4   6

Take lane from village leading to Craig-yr-iyrchen. Continue over summit, through quarry and follow forest road down to edge of reservoir. Turn left along reservoir and make for footbridge at N. end of reservoir. Do not cross footbridge, but turn sharp left and go uphill following F.P. over Mwdwl-eithin ridge, and down hill F.P. above Ty'n-y-Waen. Turn left and take F.P. back into village.

110

Clocaenog   **083543**   **3**

🅿   A   5   6

Take lane W. past church for 1 mile staying on main route at junction with road to Fron. Continue on farm and forestry track. Walk along edge of forestry plantation and take second forest road on right. Proceed direct to base of Pincyn Llys (viewpoint and monument at top). Turn right and follow farm track downhill for 1½ miles to road at Glan-yr-afon. Turn right and return to village.

111

Cyffylliog, nr.   **006547**   **8**
Ruthin

🅿   B   4   6

Not for misty weather
N. from Foel Frech crossroads by Forestry Commission tracks to

Rhyd Galed. S.W. by bridleway and path to 985544, then E. past Isgaer-wen to start.

112

Cyffylliog   **060579**   **4**

🅿   A   4   5   6

From centre of village, past church W. and turn right on F.P., over bridge and along river bank upstream for 1 mile past Nant Bach. In woodland join track and follow round to the right, uphill, to road. Turn right. After ¾ mile bear right by farm (Carreg y gath) and just beyond cattle grid, take track, left downhill to lane. Turn right and back into village.

113

Denbigh   **044653**   **2½**

🅿   ⊕   A   4   5

Take B4501 road out of Denbigh to Lawnt at 044653. Take footpath following the river to the remains of Dr. Johnson's Cottage, hence on to Dr. Johnson's monument. At this point one may cross the river and continue S. to meet the road near Pen-y-Bryn, turn left and return to Lawnt and Denbigh. (This walk is in parts along same route as Denbigh Walk from reference 050661).

114

Denbigh   **050661**   **3–5**

🅿   ⊕   A

From Denbigh S.E. via Glas Meadows Llewelyn Estate, S.W. via Galch Hill to B4501, E. to ruins of Dr. Johnson's cottage; at gate beyond, either: (a) turn right up through wood to path round Gwaenynog Hall, then E. to Galch Hill etc. (3 miles), or (b) continue to Bodeiliog Isaf; road to Gwaenynog Bach; path (starting as permissive path through farmyard) to Henllan, where turn right; take right fork (Ochr-y-Bryn) then path with wood on right, past Foxhall to cross road at 041670 and continue to Denbigh. This walk is in parts along the same route as Denbigh Walk from reference 044653

115

Gronant, nr.   **093832**
Prestatyn

🅿   A   4

From village take lane to Gwaenysgor, forking right after 1 mile, and approaching St. Elmo's Summer House by turning left to join FP above wood. From summit continue on FP across fields south-eastwards to join road leading to Llanasa. Return via road to Gwespyr, turning left after 100 yards into lane leading to Gronant.

116

Gwytherin   **876615**   **4**

🅿   A   4   5

From centre of village take lane to the N. of Inn and go W. uphill for 1 mile to top of hill. Turn left onto track crossing moor, Ffrithuchaf, and follow F.P. above small valley for 1¼ miles to road. Turn left on road and follow down into village.

117

Halkyn or   **197698**   **4**
Rhydymwyn

🅿   A   4   6

Moel-y-crio, N.W. and return by various paths over Halkyn Mountain.

118

Llanarmon-yn-Ial   **171543**   **6**

🅿   B   4   6

Boncyn y Waen-grogen, N.E. via Llyn Gweryd to beyond Plas Llanarmon, W. up valley to 168558 to pick up Offa's Dyke Path over Moel y Plâs back to start.

119

Llanbedr Dyffryn-   **161605**   **16**
Clwyd

🅿   B   6

Bwlch Pen-Barras W. and N. along field line of Clwydian Range to Nant opposite Denbigh at 121690. Return S.E. along Offa's Dyke waymarked path. Various short cuts and alternative short walks possible. (See also Moel Fammau Nature Trail).

	877675	3

From ~~river~~ ridge on Llansannan road, take F.P. on E. side of river, down river for ½ mile. Right at small stream and follow F.P. uphill past small wood, to source of stream. Continue over hill and down to road, turn right, then right at 'T' junction and first left to river bridge, Pont Sylltu. Follow F.P. over stile along W. bank of Afon Cledwen, down river to village.

121

Llannefydd	982707	3¼
P	A 4 6	

From village, take road N.; after 300 yards turn left and follow road and, later, track through gate round base of Mynydd Gaer. On W. side of the hill, go along (left) track and F.P. and up to the summit, an ancient hill fort. Take F.P. due S. and join road leading back into village.

122

Llansannan	937659	4
P	A 4 5	

From village, take F.P. (sign-posted) on E. side of River Aled, down river. Cross bridge (½ m) and continue on track and F.P. to road bridge at Bryn Rhyd yr Arian (955676). Turn left onto road and follow up hill for 1½ miles. Turn left into lane beyond woods, cross main road, and left at first cross roads, 934672, back into village.

123

Loggerheads, nr. Mold	196623	7
P	B 5 6	

Loggerheads, S. to Pentre-cerrig-mawr, W.S.W. to Llanferres, W. and S.W. skirting S. of Fron-heulog to Foel Fenlli (Iron Age fort) at 165601, N. to Bwlch Pen-Barras, N.E. through Clwyd Forest to Cwm Llydan to telephone box at 187636, cross River Alun to Leat Path back to start.

124

Melidin, nr. Prestatyn	065803	4
P	A 4 6	

Tan-yr-allt, N. along Offa's Dyke Path or lower path, return via Gwaenysgor.

125

Nannerch	171684	6
P	B 4 6	

From A541 to Firwood Farm, S.W. to Moel Arthur, E. to 162661 to pick up R.U.P.P. to Tardd-y-dwr, main road to start.

126

Prestatyn	073823	7
P	B 4 6	

073823 Park S.E. edge of town; forward uphill on road to 075821. At 2nd right swing in road go forward uphill on path with wood on right. At top of field left and right at next boundary. Over brow of hill on path to lane at 083819. Cross this lane and continue on path in same direction with wood on left. At 090819 reach sunken lane by small pond; do not enter this lane but go diagonally right over ridge to road at 094811. Turn right on surfaced lane and turn left at cross roads at 091811.

At 091805, where lane swings left, take path ahead over corner of Gop Hill to rejoin road at 092801. Right along road to A5151 at Trelawnyd at 090798; right then left by church.

At 088795, right over field to unsurfaced lane. Left and soon right to reach Marian Mill at 075790. Right and follow last 2½ miles of Offa's Dyke Path via 072797, 070799, 065803, 071810 to starting point at 073823.

127

Ruthin	122584	8
P	B 4	

From Ruthin, path N.N.E. to Rhewl, stone bridge over River Clywedog, lane and path on N.W. bank to Bontuchel; lane S. on E. side of tributary valley, forking uphill for Tyddyn Cook, path to Aberddu, road to S. of Ffordd-

Las, lane then path straight ahead, bearing left at end of hedge, lane to Llanfwrog; avoid town by paths via point marked '58' to starting point (8 miles)

128

Ruthin	126585	8
P	B 4 6	

From Ruthin roundabout (126585) road W. and path to lane beyond Wern (138592); lane beyond Plas-Tower-Bridge, path via Teiran to Bwlch-Pen-Barras and Moel Fammau. Return by Tyn-y-Celyn, Tyn-y-Caeau (130625), Plâs-yn-rhôs and near Plas Llanychan to Clwyd Bridge (120608), then path on W. bank to Ruthin. (See also Moel Fammau Nature Trail.)

129

Pentre-llyn-cymmer	973525	3½
P	A 3 5	

From village, take F.P. along S. side of Afon Alwen, downstream for 1 mile to Caer Ddunod, old castle mound. Thence, right, uphill along side of woodland for 1 mile to Hafotty Llechwedd road. Turn right on road and right again after 100 yards, through gate, on to F.P. (unmarked) leading over moor and back to village.

130

Pwll-glas	121549	3½
P	A 4 5	

Follow track from main road, S. across old railway line. Turn left, steep uphill climb along F.P. to summit of Graig-adwy-wynt, interesting limestone outcrop with remains of hill fort. At far (S.) end of ridge turn right, downhill, in front of woodland and take F.P. and green lane at side of railway track back to starting point.

131

Tremeirchion	082723	4
P	A 4 6	

Craig P.O., S.E. to 087719 and track N.E. above Sodom (do look back!) to 098723, along Offa's Dyke Path over Cefn Ddu and back by track making circuit.

Map 117
Chester

Llangollen and Wrexham

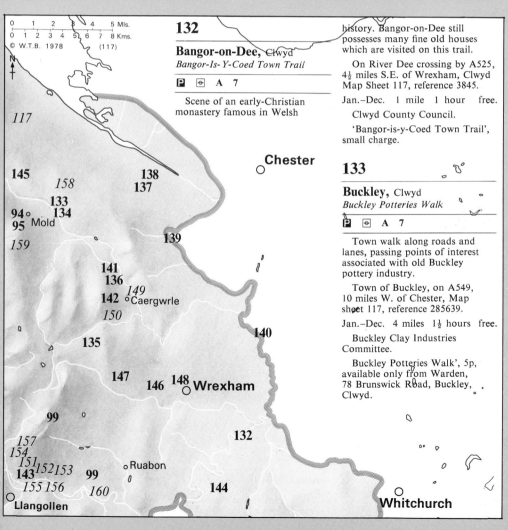

132

Bangor-on-Dee, Clwyd
Bangor-Is-Y-Coed Town Trail

P ⊕ **A 7**

Scene of an early-Christian monastery famous in Welsh

history. Bangor-on-Dee still possesses many fine old houses which are visited on this trail.

On River Dee crossing by A525, 4½ miles S.E. of Wrexham, Clwyd Map Sheet 117, reference 3845.

Jan.–Dec. 1 mile 1 hour free.

Clwyd County Council.

'Bangor-is-y-Coed Town Trail', small charge.

133

Buckley, Clwyd
Buckley Potteries Walk

P ⊕ **A 7**

Town walk along roads and lanes, passing points of interest associated with old Buckley pottery industry.

Town of Buckley, on A549, 10 miles W. of Chester, Map sheet 117, reference 285639.

Jan.–Dec. 4 miles 1½ hours free.

Buckley Clay Industries Committee.

Buckley Potteries Walk', 5p, available only from Warden, 78 Brunswick Road, Buckley, Clwyd.

27

134

Buckley, Clwyd
Buckley Town Trail

🅿 ⊕ A 7

A walk in 13 stages around the town of Buckley.

2½ miles E. of Mold on A549 Mold – Chester road. Map sheet 117, reference 279645.

Jan.–Dec. 4½ miles 3 hours free.

Buckley Elfed School and Buckley Society.

'Buckley' 5p, from District Council Offices and Clwyd County Council.

135

Bwlchgwyn, near Wrexham, Clwyd
Geological Trail

🅿 ⊕ A 7

The trail leads the visitor around a disused quarry and illustrates the geology of sedimentary rocks, fossil plants and marine shells. Faults are present with slickensides, breccia's and mineralisation. Metamorphic rocks (slate) are found in the quarry and there is evidence of the glaciation of North Wales.

Geological museum of North Wales, Bwlchgwyn. Adjacent to A525 Wrexham – Ruthin road approximately 7 miles from Wrexham on Ruthin side of Bwlchgwyn village Map sheet 117. Reference 259534.

Jan.–Dec. 1½ miles 1½ to 2 hours.

Geological Museum of North Wales. Mr. G. Stanley. Tel. Coedpoeth 571/3.

Geological Trail leaflet, 15p available from Geological Museum of North Wales gives entrance to museum.

136

Caergwrle, Clwyd
Waun-y-Llyn Country Park

🅿 A 3 6

The moorland ridge of Hope Mountain is the setting for this park beside the small lake of Waun-y-Llyn. It offers good walks, views, the lake and the study of nature.

Horeb, a hamlet on Hope Mountain, one mile west of Caergwrle, 6 miles N.W. of Wrexham. Map sheet 117, reference 288578.

Jan.–Dec. Various walks – free. from 288578 and 290565

Clwyd County Council and Countryside Commission.

137

Ewloe, Clwyd
Ewloe Castle Nature Trail

🅿 ⊕ A 4 7

Six stages explore farmland, a wooded valley and the remains of 13th century Ewloe Castle.

Cow Parsnip

Spear Thistle

Harvest Mouse

Tiger Moth

Stoat

Field Pansy

Poppy

Plantain

Sky-Lark and young

Corn Cockle

½ mile N.W. of Ewloe round-about on A55 Queensferry – Northop road. Map sheet 117, reference 292670.

Jan.–Dec. 1½ miles 1 hour free.

Clwyd County Council and Local Schools

'Ewloe Castle', 6p from H.M.S.O.
'Ewloe Castle Nature Trail', 12p.

Meadows, hay and cornfields, hedges, walls and grassy banks.

140

Holt, Clwyd
Holt past and present: A Walk

🅿 7

Site of a Roman tile-making and pottery factory, Holt is now a small country town on the Dee, crossed here by a fine 14th century bridge.

5½ miles N.E. of Wrexham, map sheet 117, reference 412545. Start from 14th century bridge over River Dee, boundary of England and Wales.

Jan.–Dec. 1½ miles 1½ hours free.

Holt Womans Institute.

'Holt past and present', 8 pp. booklet available from Womans Institute, 90 Andlon, Laburnam Way, Holt, Clwyd.

138

Ewloe, Clwyd
Wepre Park Footpath

🅿 A 5 7

No. 2 leaflet in the local councils' Quality of Life Experiment series covers the walk from Ewloe Castle to Wepre along a wooded defile.

Ewloe on A55, 2 miles S.W. of the Queensferry bridge on A494. Start at Ewloe Castle map sheet 117, reference 292673.

Jan.–Dec. 7 miles 1½ hours free.

Alyn and Deeside District Council and Clwyd County Council waymarked in yellow. Free map leaflet available.

Covers partly the same area as the Ewloe Castle Nature Trail from reference point 292670.

139

Higher Kinnerton, Clwyd
Higher Kinnerton Footpath

🅿 A 4

No. 1 leaflet in the local councils' Quality of Life Experiment series explores the Brad Brook area south of Higher Kinnerton village.

Higher Kinnerton, on by-road 1½ miles S. of Broughton. Map sheet 117, reference 328608.

Jan.–Dec. 1 mile ¾ hour free.

Alyn and Deeside District Council and Clwyd County Council.

Waymarked in yellow. Free map leaflet available.

141

Hope, Clwyd
Hope Mountain Footpath

🅿 A 6

No. 3 leaflet in the local councils' Quality of Life Experiment series explores Hope Mountain from the hamlet of Horeb.

Hope, on A550/A541, 7 miles N.W. of Wrexham. Horeb, map sheet 117, reference 288578.

Jan.–Dec. 1½ miles 1 hour free.

Alyn and Deeside District Council and Clwyd County Council.

Waymarked in yellow. Free map leaflet available.

Partly covers the area of ramble from reference 290565.

142

Llanfynydd, Clwyd
Llanfynydd Footpath

P   A   4   5

No. 4 leaflet in the local councils' Quality of Life Experiment series looks at wildlife habitats in the Black Wood of Nant y Frith valley.

Llanfynydd, on B5101, 6 miles N.W. of Wrexham. Map sheet 117, reference 279566.

Jan.–Dec.   4 miles   3 hours   free.
(alternative shorter route available)

Alyn and Deeside District Council and Clwyd County Council.

Waymarked in yellow. This footpath covers to some extent the same grounds as the ramble from reference point 284554.

143

Llangollen, Clwyd
Llangollen Town Trail

P   ⊕   A   7

A walk around this country town, famous for the Llangollen International Eisteddfod, held each year in July. St. Collen's Church and Llangollen Bridge (one of the 'Seven Wonders of Wales') are featured in the trail.

Llangollen, on A5. Map sheet 117, reference 2142.

Jan.–Dec.   1¾ miles   1 hour   free.

Clwyd County Council.

'Llangollen Town Trail', English and Cymraeg, price 30p.

144

Overton-on-Dee, Clwyd
Overton Town Trail

P   ⊕   A   7

Walk through Overton-on-Dee featuring St. Mary's Parish Church and the many interesting houses. This area has been settled for hundreds of years and reference was made to 'Ovretone' in the Domesday Book of 1086.

Overton, near east bank of River Dee on A539, 5 miles E. of Ruabon. Map sheet 117, reference 3741.

Jan.–Dec.   1 mile   ½ hour   free.

Clwyd County Council.

'Overton Town Trail', in English and Cymraeg, 15p.

145

Rhydymwyn, Clwyd
The Leat Nature Trail

P   A   3   5

Rhydymwyn Village to Trail Hill, Pontnewydd and return via Pen-y-fron. Limestone gorge features, limestone quarry with fossils, variety of trees, plants and flowers in the Alyn Valley.

Rhydymwyn, a village on A541, 2½ miles N.W. of Mold, map sheet 117, reference 206669.

Jan.–Dec.   3¾ miles   3 hours   free.

Clwyd County Council and pupils of Ysgol y Ddol, Rhydymwyn.

'Rhydymwyn Nature Trail', 5p.

146

Wrexham, Clwyd
Bersham Industrial Trail

P   ⇄   ⊕   A   3   7

In 5 miles of the Clywedog river, skirting the S. side of Wrexham, the trail visits Minera, Llwyneinion, Rhos, Bersham, Erddig Hall and King's Mills.

Clywedog river at Coedpoeth on A525, 3 miles N. of Wrexham (map sheet 117, reference 2850) to King's Mills, ¾ mile S.E. of Wrexham (map sheet 117, reference 3449).

Jan.–Dec.   5 miles   4 hours   free.

Clwyd County Council and Wrexham Borough Council.

Leaflet to be published.

147

Wrexham, Clwyd
Legacy Nature Trail

P   A   4

A study of plant and animal life recently established on man-made bunds designed to landscape an electricity substation.

On B5426 off A483 (T) south of Wrexham. Map sheet 117, reference 293484.

Jan.–Dec.   2 miles   1½ hours   free.

Central Electricity Generating Board.

By prior arrangement with District Engineer, C.E.G.B., Connah's Quay Electrical District, Connah's Quay, Deeside, Clwyd CH5 4BP. Telephone 0244 817607.

Legacy Nature Trail, 10p.

148

Wrexham, Clwyd
Wrexham Town Trail

P   ⇄   ⊕   A   7

A guide through the centre of the largest market town in North Wales, including the magnificent 15th century church and the unique triple market.

Wrexham, Clwyd, O.S. Sheet 117.

Jan.–Dec.   1 mile   20 mins.   free.

Clwyd County Council.

'Wrexham Town Trail', a booklet available locally.

Llangollen's bridge, in an area of great natural beauty.

149

Caergwrle	290565	6
P B 3 6		

Pen-rhiw, N. to Horeb and Top Rhos Farm at 283589, S. to pond in Country Park, Ty-Uchaf and back along road.

150

Ffrith, nr. Wrexham	284554	5
P A 5		

Ffrith, S.W. along path and Forestry Commission roads along N. side of Nant y Ffrith to a point 262542 opposite Bwlchgwyn. Return along path N.E. to Pen-Llan-y-gwr then to road at 273554, E. back to Ffrith.

This ramble covers in part the Llanfynydd walk from 279566.

151

Llangollen – Dinas Bran	214419	5
P ⊕ A 6		

Right from car park. Left along Castle Street and over bridge. Turn to right at bridge and sharp left up Wharf Hill and over Canal Bridge. Up steps opposite and follow F.P. signposted Castell Dinas Bran, up to castle. Walk down other side of hill along fence on right. Follow path on down to lane. Left along lane, left at gate and continue past Tan-y-Castell. 160 yards past Dinbren

Dinas Bran, mediaeval castle on a hill.

Uchaf turn sharp left and follow road for ½ mile. 100 yards past entrance to Dinbren Isaf take F.P. on left through edge of woodland. Rejoin road and continue downhill past Wylfa taking left fork down into Llangollen. (See also Dinas Bran, walk 214419 on sheet 117.)

152

Llangollen	214419	5
P ⊕ B 3 6		

Llangollen, E. along canal to A539 bridge N. to Panorama Drive road, W. to 227433, Castell Dinas Bran, S.W. back to start.

153

Llangollen	214419	8
P ⊕ B 3 6		

As previous walk to 236427, path goes off N. of A539, path E. to Trevor Uchaf, Plas Ifa, Trevor Hall, Offa's Dyke Path to Castell Dinas Bran and back to start.

154

Llangollen	214419	7
P ⊕ A 3 5		

N.W. along canal to Pentrefelin, Valle Crucis Abbey N.W. to 202445, road used as public footpath (R.U.P.P.) over National Trust land, S. to Chain Bridge, (sheet 125) at 198433, cross A5 to 204434 from which roads and paths lead to Llangollen.

155

Llangollen	219417	8–10
P ⊕ B 3 5 6		

Llangollen, E. to Ty-Uchaf, through 236409 and 260409 to Pen-y-graig, Froncysyllte, N. over aqueduct, either follow canal back to Llangollen or take Offa's Dyke Path via Trevor Hall to Castell Dinas Bran and back.

156

Llangollen	219417	7
P ⊕ B 4 6		

Llangollen to 236409 as on previous walk then divert S.E. to

253404, lanes S. to Pennant (to map 126) Garth Obry, Grogwen Wladys, Castle Mill, Bronygarth, river paths to Chirk for bus to Llangollen.

157

Llangollen	233478	3
P A 5 6		

World's End, S. along Offa's Dyke Path to track at 224473, whence N.E. through rocks, S. and E. of woods to 237477 and back through woods to start.

158

Mold	235660	6
P ⊕ B 4		

½ mile S.W. of Soughton (Sychdyn), N. to 235677, Soughton Farm, Northop, S.E. to Soughton Hall, S.W. to N. of the Laurels, back to start.

159

Maeshafn, nr. Mold	202610	4
P A 5 6		

Starts and ends on sheet 117 but route is substantially on sheet 116. S.W. to Pot Hole return up valley by roads or paths via Pant-du to start.

160

Pontcysyllte	272423	3
P ⊕ A 3		

Park car on towing path. Follow path across the Telford Aqueduct and along the canal side to the Swing Bridge. Cross canal and turn right. Join road opposite Argoed Hall (271419) and follow road to the right past Argoed Farm and across the mediaeval Cysyllte Bridge. Turn left along valley road for approximately ½ mile past Trevor Cottage and the 17th century farmhouse, Plas-yn-y-Pentre. Turn right up steep narrow lane and join canal. Follow canal N.E. to B5434 turn left for 140 yards then over canal bridge and sharp right into towing path. (See also walk 219417 on sheet 117).

Map 123
Lleyn Peninsula

Lleyn Peninsula

161

Llanystumdwy, Gwynedd
Talhenbont (Eisteddfod) Walk

🅿 A 3 5

Explores the narrow and wooded valley of the Dwyfor in Lloyd-George country. It has a large number of tree species.

¾ mile N. of Llanystumdwy on A497, near Gwynfryn Plas. Map sheet 123, reference 468386.

Jan.–Dec.   1 mile   1 hour   free.

Forestry Commission.

Waymarked only.

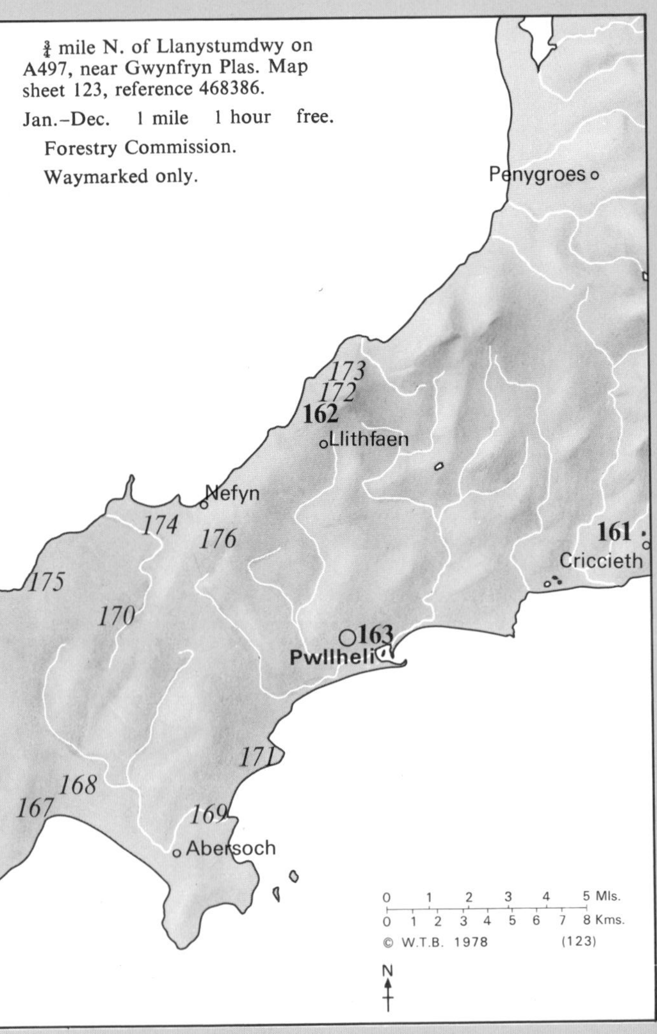

Penygroes ○

173
172
162
○ Llithfaen

○ Nefyn

174
176

175

170

161 .
Criccieth

○**163**
Pwllheli ○

171

168
167   169

165   ○ Aberdaron   ○ Abersoch
164
166

0   1   2   3   4   5 Mls.
0   1   2   3   4   5   6   7   8 Kms.
© W.T.B. 1978   (123)

N
↑

162

Llithfaen, Gwynedd
Ty Canol Walk

P A 1 5 6

The remarkable coastal mountain, ¾ mile north of Llithfaen, is wooded, with views over Caernarfon Bay, giving exciting walking country.
¾ mile N. of Llithfaen on B4417 extension of the Caernarfon – Nefyn road. Map sheet 123, reference 353440. Start at the picnic site.
Jan.–Dec. ½ mile 1 hour free.
Forestry Commission.
Waymarked only.

163

Pwllheli, Gwynedd
Pwllheli Town and Country Trails

P ⬛ ⊕ A 4 7

Two trails – the town trail explores the streets and walks of Pwllheli; the country trail looks at the River Rhydhir's lower waters and the footpaths that circle the town.
Pwllheli, Map sheet 123, reference 375349.
Town Trail
Jan.–Dec. ½ mile ¾ hour free.
Country Trail
Jan.–Dec. 3 miles 1–2 hours free.
Pwllheli and District Round Table.
Free booklet published by Pwllheli Round Table available from Information Centre, Pwllheli (See back of this booklet).

164

Aberdaron	140260	3

P A 1

From car park on Mynydd Mawr 2½ miles S.W. of Aberdaron follow coast S. past Ffynnon Fair to Porth Felen and back over headland.

165

Aberdaron	155264	5

P A 1

From point 1¼ miles W. of Aberdaron go N. to Anelog and back to start along coast via Llanllawen.

166

Aberdaron	155254	4

P A 1

From point 1½ miles S.W. of Aberdaron on main road near Bodermid go W. then S. to Garreg Fawr, E. on path with spur to Pen y Cil (National Trust), along coast to Porth Meudwy and back to start.

167

Aberdaron: Y Rhiw	228277	6

P B 5 6

From the village go E.N.E. through wood to 242300 at Gallt-traeth, then N.W. to 234305 and back over top of Mynydd Rhiw via Stone Age Axe factory.

168

Aberdaron: Y Rhiw	228277	3

P A 1

From the village walk E.S.E. to path near cliffs at Graig-Ddu then S.S.W. over National Trust coast land to ref. 225265 then N.N.E. along top of rocky escarpment to start.

169

Abersoch	314282	5

P A 1 2

Abersoch, turn left down Lon Golff, ¼ mile along Sarn road S. from Abersoch, to Golf Links on to Porth Tocyn at 324265 return W. to Sarn Bach. Return to Abersoch by same route, avoiding road.

170

Dinas, nr. Tudweiliog	267355	6–8

P B 6

From Nant Llaniestyn S.E. to Garn and circle Carn Fadryn and/or Garn Bach. Ancient road in valley between 2 peaks leads to encampment on Carn Fadryn.

171

Llanbedrog	331315	3

P A 1

S.E. past church at Llanbedrog for the footpath around Mynydd Tir y Cwmwd and back.

172

Llithfaen	345429	5

P B 3 6

From ¾ mile W. of Llithfaen follow path N. to Porth y Nant and back via the headland of Penrhyn Glas.

173

Llithfaen	354442	3

P A 1 5

From the Forestry Commission's car park at Mount Pleasant go N.E. along Graig Ddu before dropping sharply W. by footpath to old village at Nant Gwrtheyrn. Return by zigzag path through young forest plantation to Mount Pleasant car park.

174

Morfa Nefyn	282407	2

P A 2 3

Along sands and paths to Porth Dinllaen Lifeboat Station, back along track.

175

Rhos-y-llan, Tudweiliog	233375	4

P A 3

Track to cliffs then N.E. along coast path to Borth Wen near Porth Dinllaen Golf Course, Morfa Nefyn, or S. to Porth Witlin with several intermediate points of access back to road.

176

Tanygraig, nr. Nefyn	315386	6

P B 6

From near Tanygraig N.W. and N. to summit of Garn Boduan, back to 318390 to circle anti-clockwise to Nefyn, and S. to Allt Garn and back to starting point.

Map 124
Dolgellau

Dolgellau

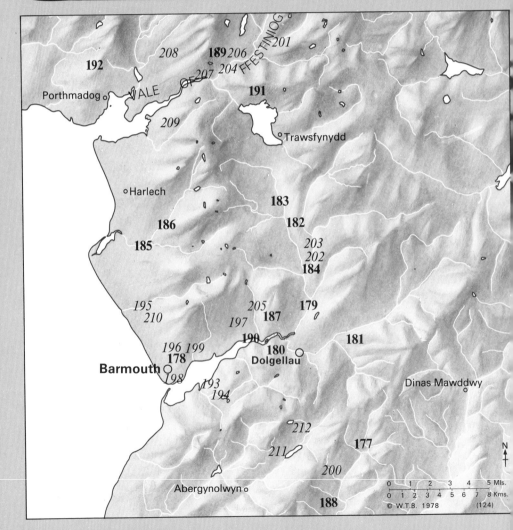

192

208 189 206 201
207 204 FFESTINIOG
Porthmadog VALE OF
191
209
Trawsfynydd
Harlech
183
186 182
203
185 202
184
195 205 179
210 197 187
190
196 199 181
178 180
Barmouth Dolgellau
198
193 Dinas Mawddwy
194
212
177
211
200 N
Abergynolwyn 0 1 2 3 4 5 Mls.
0 1 2 3 4 5 6 7 8 Kms.
188 © W.T.B. 1978 (124)

177

Aberllefenni, Gwynedd
Foel Friog Forest Trail

P A 5

A waymarked trail from Foel Friog picnic place of seven stages in the Dyfi Forest, an area of considerable beauty. A special booklet produced by the Forestry Commission interprets the scene and makes some suggestions for its better enjoyment and understanding.

Aberllefenni, 1 mile N.E. of Corris. Map sheet 124, reference 769092.

Jan.–Dec. 1½ miles 2 hours free.

Forestry Commission.

'Foel Friog Forest Trail', 5p.

178

Barmouth, Gwynedd
Panorama Walk

P ⇄ ⊕ B 6

A truly panoramic walk, 4 miles in length offering superb views of the Mawddach Estuary, the Cader range to the south and Diffwys to the north. Return along A496.

Off A496 Barmouth – Dolgellau road, 100 yards E. of railway bridge. Map sheet 124, reference 620158.

Jan.–Dec. 4 miles 3 hours free.

Cader Idris, 2927 feet high mountain on Cardigan Bay.

179

Dolgellau, Gwynedd
Precipice Walk

P B 6

A steep walk encircling high ridge offering superb views of Cader Idris, Mawddach Estuary and Snowdonia beyond.

2¾ miles north of Dolgellau, off Llanfachreth road towards Ty'n-y-Groes. Map sheet 124, reference 745213.

Jan.–Dec. 3 miles 2 hours free.

Snowdonia National Park.

'The Precipice Walk', 4p.

180

Dolgellau, Gwynedd
Talywaen Farm Trail

P A 4 6

Talywaen is private land high above Mawddach Estuary on the flanks of Cader Idris mountain. Views are splendid. Beside the walk there are picnic sites, ponies and play area. Dogs must be left in kennels at the car park.

Dolgellau on A493 and A470. Talywaen lies S.W. on Cader Road. Map sheet 124, reference 698172.

Jan.–Dec. 2 mls. 2½ hrs. £1 per car.

H.G. Humphreys, Talywaen Farm, Dolgellau. Tel. (0341) 422580.

Brochure available on site.

181

Dolgellau, Gwynedd
Torrent Walk

P A 3 5

A scenic walk along the shaded bank of the River Clywedog, with its many waterfalls.

Off A470, 2 miles East of Dolgellau, on B4416 Brithdir road. Map sheet 124, reference 761178.

Jan.–Dec. 1 mile 1 hour free.

General access but land private.

182

Ganllwyd, Gwynedd
Dolgefeiliau Forest Trail

P A 5

A woodland trail, in 3 loops,

½ mile, 1½ mile, 2 miles, waymarked in blue, red, yellow.

Off A470 at Pont Dolgefeiliau, 5 miles N. of Dolgellau. Map sheet 124, reference 722268.

Jan.–Dec. 2 miles 1½ hours free.

Forestry Commission.

Recreation Forester, Maesgwm Centre, Ganllwyd.

'Dolgefeiliau Forest Trail', 5p.

183

Ganllwyd, Gwynedd
Maesgwm Forest Visitor Centre and Coed y Brenin Forest Walks

P A B C 5

The centre provides an introduction to the forest and the life and work of its community. Within the forest there are 50 miles of waymarked walks, clearly identified on a map available at the centre.

8 miles N. of Dolgellau on A470, map sheet 124, reference 721269.

Jan.–Dec. Various walks – free.

Forestry Commission.

Forest guide and map, 25p.

Centre open Easter to October.

Lady's smock

184

Ganllwyd, Gwynedd
Ty'n-y-Groes Forest Trail

P A 5

Two-mile forest walk illustrating trees, plants and wildlife within Coed-y-Brenin Forest. Alternative shorter route (1 mile).

Ganllwyd, 5 miles N. of Dolgellau off A470. Map sheet 124, reference 730233.

Jan.–Dec. 2 miles 1½ hours free

Forestry Commission.

'Ty'n-y-Groes Forest Trail', 10p.

Llanbedr, Near Harlech, Gwynedd
Cefn Isaf Farm Trail

P A 4

A 2 mile circuit explaining the working of a typical Welsh hill farm situated above Cwm Bychan.

4 miles S.E. of Harlech, off A496 at Llanbedr. Map sheet 124, reference 603273.

Jan.–Dec. 2 miles 1½ hours free.

Snowdonia National Park.

186

Llanbedr, Near Harlech, Gwynedd
Cwm Nantcol Nature Trail

P A 5 6

A short riverside walk showing how nature has moulded the landscape. Plaques en route.

4 miles S.E. of Harlech, off A496 at Llanbedr, on Cwm Nantcol road. Map sheet 124, reference 607270.

Jan.–Dec. ½ mile ½ hour free.

Snowdonia National Park.

187

Llanelltyd, Near Dolgellau, Gwynedd
New Precipice Walk

P B 6

A high level path overlooking the beautiful Mawddach Estuary, with views of Cader Idris.

Start: Foel Ispri farm car park on a side-road off A496 Llanelltyd – Barmouth road from Pen-y-bryn. Map sheet 124, reference 698201.

Jan.–Dec. 2 miles 2 hours free.

Private but expected to be waymarked by Snowdonia National Park Authority from 1978.

188

Machynlleth, Powys
Tan-y-coed Forest Walk, Corris

P B 5

2 mile forest walk through Dovey Forest (yellow signs). Shorter route available (red signs).

4 miles N. of Machynlleth, off A487. Map sheet 124, reference 756054. Start at Tan-y-coed picnic site.

Jan.–Dec. 2 miles 2 hours free.

Forestry Commission.

'Tan-y-coed Forest Walk', 10p.

189

Maentwrog, Gwynedd
Coed Llyn Mair Nature Trail

P A 5

Oak woodlands and meadows overlooking a small lake visited by blackheaded gulls, mallards and little grebes with occasional goldeneye and whooper swans in winter.

On B4410 Maentwrog – Rhyd road, off A470, map sheet 124, reference 652416

Easter to 2–3 miles 1½ hours free. Sept.

Nature Conservancy.

'Coed Llyn Mair Nature Trail', 5p.

190

Penmaenpool, Gwynedd
Penmaenpool to Morfa Mawddach Walk

P A 2

From the former signal box at Penmaenpool, now a small exhibition point and bird observatory, the walk follows the path of the former railway along the previously inaccessible shore of the beautiful Mawddach Estuary.

Penmaenpool, map sheet 124, reference 693184 to Morfa Mawddach, map sheet 124, reference 628142.

Jan.–Dec. 7 miles 2½ hours free.

Snowdonia National Park.

Warden at Penmaenpool.

191

Trawsfynydd, Gwynedd
Trawsfynydd Nature Trail

P A 3

Three-mile circuit along shore of Llyn Trawsfynydd.

Trawsfynydd Power Station, off A470. Map sheet 124, reference 384698.

Jan.–Dec. 3 miles 1½–2 hours free.

Central Electricity Generating Board.

'Trawsfynydd Nature Trail', 5p.

192

Tremadog, Gwynedd
Tremadog Trail

P 🚌 ♿ A 2

The trail demonstrates the importance of nature conservancy and biological research in this area.

Tremadog, map sheet 124, reference 562400, ½ mile south of the A487/A498 junction.

Start and finish along the track by the side of the church, following the clearly marked arrows.

Jan.–Dec. 1 mile 1¼ hours. free.

The Christian Mountain Centre, Tremadog.

Birthplace of Lawrence of Arabia.

Booklet in course of preparation.

193

Arthog	637142	13

P C 6

From 637142 E. up B.R. to old road turning S. and S.W. to 601081 N. to Llwyngwril, return by lower track via 610109 to 636130, then N.E. to drop to start.

194

Arthog	637142	13

P C 6

From 637142 E. up B.R. to old road turning S. and S.W. to 635115 where turn S.S.E. dropping to Castell y Bere, follow road then B.R. N.N.E. to 692135. Turn W. and follow tracks on top of Craig-las to about 669127 when drop N.W. to join path which joins road just W. of Hafotty-fach, turn L. for ½ m where a track leads to the route down.

195

Barmouth/ Talybont	590218	8

P 🚌 ♿ B 6

Bus Barmouth to Talybont, 590218 E.N.E. to Pont Fadog,

S.E. to Bwlch y Rhiwgyr (Pass) then S. via Bwlch-y-llan and Garn Gorllwyn to Barmouth.

196

Barmouth	613158	5

P ☰ ⊕ B 1 6

From Barmouth climb to Dinas Oleu the National Trust's first property, then on to Garn Gorllwyn descending via footpaths to the E. end of Barmouth.

197

Barmouth	613158	6

P ⊕ B 6

Bus or car along A496 to Bontddu. Walk N.W. along road via 668197 (telephone box) to path travelling W. through Uwch-mynydd and skirting forest to Bwlch y Rhywgyr. Take path S. to Bwlch y Llan and then through National Trust's Dinas Oleu to Barmouth.

198

Barmouth	618156	3

P ☰ A 2

Barmouth to Morfa Mawddach on the estuary's S. side via toll viaduct or ferry to Penrhyn Point.

199

Barmouth	618156	5

P ☰ ⊕ A 1 6

'Panorama Walk' from Barmouth (Porkington Terrace). Waymarked.

200

Corris	755077	6

P B 5 6

From 755077 on A487 in Corris take F.P. at corner down to the village and the bridge which cross and go S. In a short time take F.P. N.N.E. to Aberllefenni from where take path in N.W. direction up the side valley to Hengae from where a faintly defined track leads W. uphill towards Ceiswyn. On reaching open country follow the ridge over Mynydd Hafoty in a S. direction to join track at 744097 for Upper Corris and minor road back to Corris.

201

Ffestiniog	701419	8

P ☰ ⊕ B 3 6

Ffestiniog N. towards Youth Hostel, turn W. along to Cwm Teigl – Rhyd y Sarn. Cross Afon Teigl and Afon Goedel for sharp climb to Dduallt, descend to Pont Talybont and climb the Cynfal Valley to Rhaeadr Cynfal returning N.W. and N. to Ffestiniog.

202

Ganllwyd	727243	2

P A 3 5

N.W. along N. bank of Afon Gamlan from Ganllwyd to the waterfall of Rhaeadr Ddu returning through the woods on the S. bank.

203

Ganllwyd	727243	7

P B 3 5

Pont ar Eden N.E. on W. bank of Afon Mawddach to waterfalls of Pistyll Cain and Rhaeadr Mawddach, return on E. bank or through forests to Ganllwyd.

204

Gellilydan, nr. Maentwrog	676400	4

P A 3 5

S. and W. to Rhaeadr Du (waterfall), up river to track to Llwyn and back to start.

205

Llanelltyd	690192	3

P A 5 6

From Pen-y-bryn 1¾ miles W. of Llanelltyd on A496 road go up Cwmmynach N. about ¾ mile, take road N.E. and S. to 697200, skirt Foel Ispri (New Precipice Walk) E. to 718200 above Llanelltyd to return along lower path.

206

Maentwrog	650410	4

P ☰ A 5

Llyn Mair (653413) or Tanybwlch, tracks through Coed Ty-coch to Dduallt, a lovely old farm near the narrow gauge railway. Drop down hill to road for return.

207

Maentwrog	654396	4

P A 6

Ivy Bridge, 1¼ miles on A496 S.W. of Maentwrog, track to Llyn Tecwynuchaf, E. to 658388 then N.N.W. to start.

208

Rhyd, nr. Penrhyn-deudraeth	636420	5

P B 6

From Rhyd, S.W. towards Penrhyndeudraeth and back by almost parallel path through Coed Llyn y Garnedd.

209

Talsarnau	628370	3

P A 3 6

From Llyn Tecwyn Isaf (628371) head N.E. via Llandecwyn Church to Llyn Tecwyn Uchaf returning along roadway from 648380 to starting point.

210

Talybont	589218	5

P ☰ ⊕ B 6

E.N.E. via Llecheiddior to Pont Fadog then crossing Afon Ysgethin N.W. to Cors y Gedol burial chamber before turning S. at 597228 along path to R.U.P.P. which runs along valley to Talybont. (See also walk from reference 590218).

211

Talyllyn	716103	8

P B 6

From 716103 track from Pentre Dolamarch over stream (BR) and W. and N.W. to Pencoed drop to Llanfihangel-y-Pennant. E. to 687083, N.E. to outward path at Rhiwogof.

212

Talyllyn	730114	3

P B 6

From 730114 follow path up stream to Llyn Cau and back.

Map 125
Bala and Lake Vyrnwy

Bala and Lake Vyrnwy

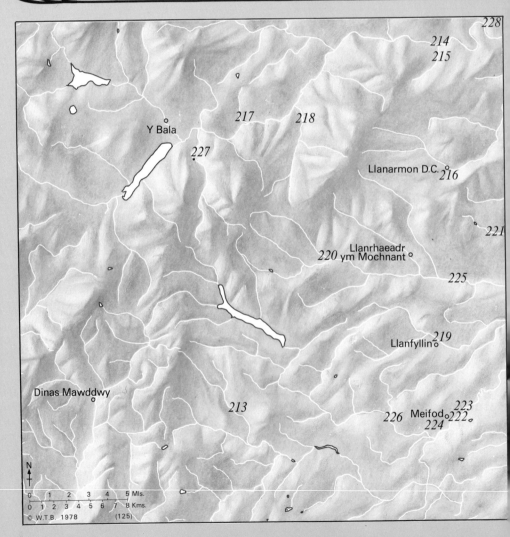

228

214
215

217   *218*

Y Bala

227

Llanarmon D.C. *216*

221

Llanrhaeadr
220 ym Mochnant

225

219
Llanfyllin

Dinas Mawddwy

213

Llanfyllin

226 Meifod *223*
222
224

N

| 0 | 1 | 2 | 3 | 4 | 5 Mls. |
| 0 | 1 | 2 | 3 | 4 | 5 | 6 | 7 | 8 Kms. |

© W.T.B. 1978   (125)

213

Foel	973145	6
P B 3 4		

Go W.N.W. through woods towards Bryniau, N. to Llechog and beyond to bridge, return E. side of Afon Twrch to 980153, back to start via Pen-y-coed.

214

Glyndyfrdwy	148426	10
P C 5 6		

S. along E. side of Nant y Pandy to Nant, follow old tramway, S. and S.W. to 123400, N. to Nant Ffriddisel woods and Forestry Commission tracks to Carrog and R.U.P.P. E. to start.

215

Glyndyfrdwy	148426	5
P B 5 6		

Through gate – follow stream up E. side past Tan-y-Turnpath, Pandy and disused slate quarry o Nant. Sharp left at fork for mile to join track. Turn sharp right and climb with track for over a mile to near summit. Turn left down bridle path over moor through woodland, past Tyn-y-Graig, Tyn-y-Llwyn, Dreboeth and Siambr Wen. Join classified road above school. Left along A5, down hill to start.

216

Llanarmon Dyffryn Ceiriog	158329	3½
A 6		

Take road to Llanrhaeadr for mile at sharp bend in road follow footpath left uphill to meet track on top of Cefn Hir-fynydd 159313) ridge. Turn left to next hill, bearing left where tracks meet at 173323. Drop to 176335 and return to village along footpath.

217

Llandderfel	982371	9
C 6		

Road N.E. to Garth-lwyd R.U.P.P. E.N.E. and track E. to Tyn-y-graig, road E. and N.E.

218

to Tyfos and R.U.P.P. N.W. to 018401, bridleway S.W. to Cistfaen, track and road back.

Llandrillo	036371	9
P C 6		

Hard walk – do not undertake in mist

Bridge in village S. and E.S.E. to Bwlch Maen Gwynedd, back N.W. to 051376, then W. to start.

219

Llanfyllin	143196	2
P A 4 5		

From bridge on Llangedwyn road, E. to Green Hall hill and back by S. route.

220

Llangynog	033253	4
P A 3 6		

From Rhydfelin go W.S.W. past Pwlliago, follow stream to Llyn y Mynydd.

221

Llansilin	209283	5½
P B 3 6		

Park in the village and take the narrow road leading to Moelfre Lake (which is privately owned) a distance of some 2 miles; to avoid the main road turn right at 204281 and walk by lanes and footpaths past Pentre to the road at 188283. Follow around the N.E. side of the lake to the road junction near Fron, turn right and take the F.P. past Fron climbing over Gyrn Moelfre to Moeliwrch, thence continue E. for nearly half a mile to meet the road to Llansilin. Turn right and return to the village.

222

Meifod	153132	4
P B 4 6		

Meifod to Gallt yr Ancr, S.W. to 142125, N.W. then N.E. to Allt fawr, E. to Goetre and return to start.

223

Meifod	153143	4
P A 5 6		

From start take paths and Forestry Commission roads anti-clockwise around Allt y Main.

224

Meifod	158127	5
P A 3 4		

Meifod Bridge, E. to bridleway towards Pant Glas but turn right to Llyn Du, exit from wood well W. of Llyn Du. Return to road alongside Llyn Du, follow road to Fron-las, path to near Clawdd-llesg, road past Lower Hall to path to river which follow to bridge.

225

Pentrefelin	155243	6
P B 4 5		

Park car by river bridge and follow bridle path E. through edge of woodland to Fron Goch. Thence along contour track and road down to hamlet of Bwlchyddar. Turn sharp right just before main road and follow lane uphill to Mynydd y Glyn. Turn right on gated track past Croniarth Farm, downhill to Glantanat Isaf (note Motte, or Castle mound) and back to river bridge.

226

Pontrobert, near Meifod	095138	5
P A 4 5		

W. through woods then N. towards Dolwar Hall, to 075148, W. to Halfren and back to start.

227

Rhos-y-gwaliau, near Bala	943346	6
P B 6		

S.E. through Bryncut to Maeshir, N. then N.W. to Ty Isaf at 963354 then W. to start.

Valle Crucis	199434	4

🅿 A 3 5

From car park above Chain Bridge Hotel down steps and footbridge to canal. Turn left and follow canal to Pentrefelin (207437). Left over canal bridge, right along A542 for 100 yards. Cross road opposite white cottage and follow footpath across two fields below rifle range keeping to right hand hedge. Take track down to left across footbridge to Abbey at 205442. (Former Cistercian Monastery.) F.P. to A452 at Abbey Dingle. Turn right along A542 for ¼ mile to Eliseg's Pillar. Retrace steps to telephone kiosk.

For flat walking, follow lane to right for 1 mile joining road at Bryntysilio Lodge. For more strenuous walking cross stile and follow path through Coed Hyddyn over Velvet Hill to Bryntysilio Lodge (½ mile). Follow road along to right to Llantysilio Church at 193436. Turn left through gate and along F.P. to Horseshoe Falls. Follow path along canal behind Chain Bridge Hotel up second footbridge to car park.

Jackdaw

Habitats that include places of architectural or historic interest.

Young Rabbits

Bramble

Jackdaw

Bramble

41

Map 126
Shrewsbury

Chirk and Welshpool

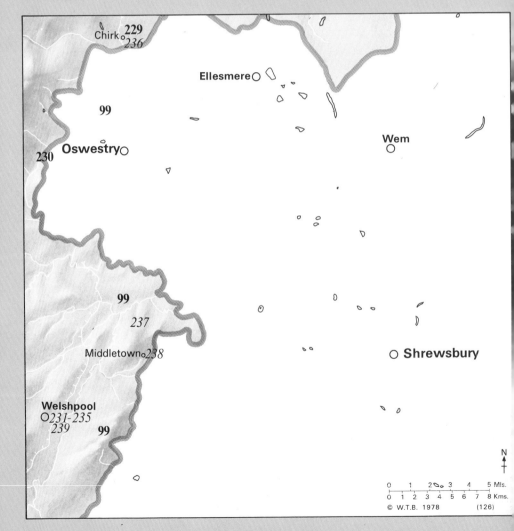

Chirk **229**
236

Ellesmere○

99

Oswestry○

230

Wem
○

99

237

Middletown○*238*

Welshpool
○*231-235*
239 **99**

○ Shrewsbury

N
↑

| 0 | 1 | 2 | 3 | 4 | 5 Mls. |
| 0 | 1 | 2 | 3 | 4 | 5 | 6 | 7 | 8 Kms. |

© W.T.B. 1978 (126)

229

Chirk, Clwyd
Llangollen Canal Trail

🅿 B 3 7

Attractive walk along a ten mile section of a rural canal through an area of great natural beauty and crossing Telford's aqueduct, the most famous and spectacular feature of Britain's canal system.

Llangollen Canal from Chirk to Llangollen. Map sheet 126, reference 284378.

Jan.–Dec. 10 miles* 5 hours free.

Clwyd County Council in conjunction with British Waterways Board.

'Llangollen Canal Trail', small charge.

*Shorter sections can be taken.

230

Tanat Valley, Clwyd
Motor and Village Trails around Llangedwyn, Llanrhaeadr-ym-Mochnant, Llansilin

🅿 A 7

Tour by car around the green valleys of the Border country between the Dee and Severn. Then absorb the timeless, peaceful air of its little villages and historic places.

Start at Llansilin on Llanhaeadr-ym-Mochnant road, S4580, 6 miles W. of Oswestry. Map sheet 126, reference 209284.

Jan.–Dec. 15 miles 2 hours free.
  by car
  1 mile
  walking

Clwyd County Council.

'Tanat Valley', brochure (small charge).

231

Welshpool	218075	5

🅿 🚲 ⊕ B 4 6

From lane left of The Raven pub at 218075 go W.S.W. 2½ miles by paths past Talyrnau to road under hill fort at 181059. N.E. to Sylfaen railway station, W. on A458 for 150 yards to path N.

from stile near Sylfaen cottage to Y Golfa at 186070, then E. through Llanerchyddol Hall to Welshpool.

232

Welshpool	224076	6

🅿 🚲 ⊕ B 4 6

From Town Hall via Hall Street footpath N. from side of Workingmen's Club to Coedylade (222091) N. by path and lane to join B4392 ½ mile S. of Guilsfield. Return E. 1 mile to The Coppice S. then S.E. via Trelydan to Yr Allt at 238097 for paths S. arriving at Welshpool by The Flash pond and high school, Bronwylfa Road.

233

Welshpool	228073	5

🅿 🚲 ⊕ B 4 6

S. from Ysgol Maesydre, primary school, by swimming baths in Howell Drive by path E. then W. side of railway to 227042, W. by footpath (crossing A483) to canal bridge at 200045, N.E. to Powis Park, enter at 220061 for path to town.

234

Welshpool	228075	9

🅿 🚲 ⊕ B 4 6

From car park take path S.E. between Bowling Club and saw mill and S.E. of river via The White House to B4388 at 238053. Climb E. past pools in dingle to 254047 then N.E. to Beacon Ring fort (265058) to join Offa's Dyke Path to Buttington Bridge (246089), returning along canal bank to town. (Note: This walk traverses part of area covered by walk on map sheet 126, reference 245060.)

235

Welshpool	232084	6

🅿 🚲 ⊕ B 4 6

High School in Bronwylfa Road N.E. past The Flash pond along paths, through wickets and stiles to lane along W. side of Yr Allt, passing Coppice Farm, through Dyer's Farm down to canal at 256116, along Offa's Dyke by canal side to cross canal from 238083.

236

Chirk	263377	2

🅿 A 3 4

Castle Mill on B4500, Offa's Dyke going N.W. then N.E. over fields. Right on summer only permissive path by Home Farm, under Chirk Castle and right to Castle Mill (O.D.A.)

237

Criggion	294149	5

🅿 A 5 6

E. up track to bridleway running S.E., out of wood and on to road near Belle Eisle Farm, over Middletown Hill, cross valley at 297132, go N.E. and N. to 295141 to reach Rodney's Pillar and back to start.

238

Middletown	283119	5

🅿 A 4 6

Start near Garreg Bank, E. and N. up Moel y Golfa, down to The Dingle, N.N.W. to New Pieces, Upper Farm, tracks and paths to start. Alternatively from The Dingle return by path on S.E. side of Moel y Golfa.

239

Welshpool	218075	4

🅿 🚲 ⊕ A 4 6

From The Raven pub at 218075 go W. through Llanerchyddol Hall paths to 203076, diverging N.W. along paths near Frocha Common and Ty brith to 198091. Return E. via Cloddiau, Groespluen to A490.

Map 135
Aberystwyth

Aberystwyth

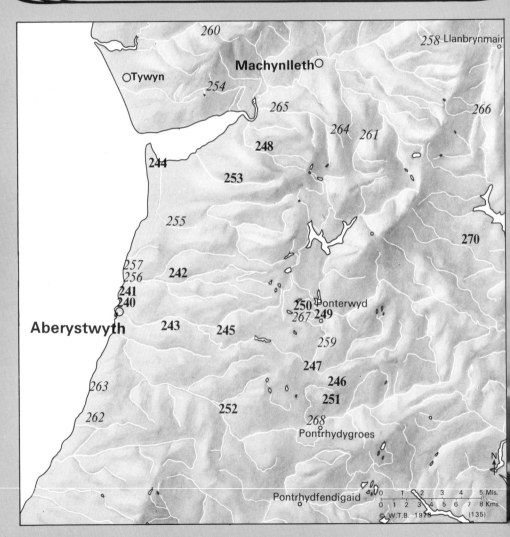

260

258 Llanbrynmair

Machynlleth○

○Tywyn

254

265

266

264   261

248

244

253

255

270

257
256
242

241
240

Aberystwyth

250 ○Ponterwyd
267 249

243   245

259

247

263

246

251

262

252

268
Pontrhydygroes

N

Pontrhydfendigaid

0 1 2 3 4 5 Mls.
0 1 2 3 4 5 6 7 8 Kms.
© W.T.B. 1978   (135)

44

240

Aberystwyth, Dyfed
Aberystwyth Town Trail

P ⇆ ⊕ A 7

Thirty-three interesting buildings and places in the town of Aberystwyth visited on a town trail around this Cardigan Bay seaside resort.

Aberystwyth, between the station harbour and sea front. Map sheet 135, reference 584815.

Jan.–Dec. 2 miles 2 hours free.

Welsh Arts Council, for European Architectural Heritage Year.

'Llwybr Tref Aberystwyth/ Aberystwyth Town Trail', small charge, available locally.

241

Aberystwyth, Dyfed
Constitution Hill Nature Trail

P ⇆ ⊕ A 1

Two walks on the hills and cliffs north from Aberystwyth with fine views over Cardigan Bay and the Plynlimon range.

Aberystwyth's seafront starts at Constitution Hill where there is a Nature Trail.

242

Aberystwyth, Dyfed
Gogerddan Forest Walk

P A 5

An effortless but interesting walk through woodlands and Arboretum near Plas Gogerddan.

3 miles N. of Aberystwyth, off A4159. Map sheet 135, reference 632838.

Jan.–Dec. 1 mile 1 hour free.

Forestry Commission.

Waymarked.

Constitution Hill, N. end of promenade, Aberystwyth. Map sheet 135, reference 584823.

Jan.–Dec.   free.

Short trail 1 mile $\frac{3}{4}$ hour
Long trail 3 miles $2\frac{1}{2}$ hours

West Wales Naturalists' Trust.

'Constitution Hill Nature Trail', 32p.

243

Aberystwyth, Dyfed
Vale of Rheidol Railway Nature Trail

P ⇆ ⊕ A 4 5

Though not strictly a walk, this fascinating trail will certainly invite walking at each of the stations, and particularly at Devil's Bridge.

Aberystwyth, Dyfed. Map sheet 135.

Rail journey of 12 miles from Aberystwyth to Devil's Bridge with walking from intermediate stations.

British Rail and West Wales Naturalists' Trust.

'What to see in the Vale of Rheidol', 29p available from British Rail Station, Aberystwyth.

244

Borth, Dyfed,
Ynyslas Nature Trail

P A 2

A duneland trail of great interest revealing the flora and fauna of the Ynyslas Nature Reserve.

On Dovey Estuary, 7 miles N. of Aberystwyth off B4572. Map sheet 135, reference 610940.

Jan.–Dec. 1½ miles 1 hour free.

Nature Conservancy.

'Ynyslas Nature Trail' 5p.

245

Capel Bangor, Near Aberystwyth, Dyfed
Cwmrheidol Nature Trail

P ⇆ A 3 4

Encircling reservoir, the trail features birds, plants and trees en route.

Cwmrheidol, off A44 at Capel Bangor, 5 miles E. of Aberystwyth. Map sheet 135, reference 698796.

Jan.–Dec. 2½ miles 2 hours free.

Central Electricity Generating Board.

The Superintendent, Rheidol Power Station.

'Cwm Rheidol Nature Trail,' 5p.

246

Cwmystwyth, Devil's Bridge
Dyfed
Arch Forest Trail

🅿 A 5

Forest trail, 1½ miles long through plantations. Viewpoint. Shorter routes (1 mile and ½ mile) marked.

Off B4574 Cwmystwyth – Devil's Bridge road at The Arch, a memorial to King George III. Map sheet 135, reference 765756.

Jan.–Dec. 1½ miles 1 hour free.

Forestry Commission.

'The Arch Forest Trail', 5p.

Bilingual Signs mark Forestry Commission picnic sites.

247

Devil's Bridge, Dyfed
Devil's Bridge Nature Trail

🅿 ♿ A 5

Waterfalls and wooded gorge scenery, seen from some rather steep steps and paths below the hotel at Devil's Bridge.

Off A4120 at junction with B4574, at Devil's Bridge. Map sheet 135, reference 742771.

Jan.–Dec. 1 mile 45 minutes 20p.

Crest Hotels Ltd., c/o Hafod Arms Hotel, Devil's Bridge.

To be re-published shortly by Crest Hotels Ltd.

248

Machynlleth, Powys
Taliesin Forest Walk

🅿 A 5

Forest walk in Artist's Valley. Explanation Boards en route

1 mile inland from Furnace, off A487 Machynlleth – Aberystwyth road Map sheet 135, reference 692945.

Jan.–Dec. 1 mile ¾ hour free.

Forestry Commission.

249

Ponterwyd, Dyfed
(a) Bwlch Nant-yr-arian Forest Trail
(b) Jubilee Walk

🅿 A 5 6

Steep, wooded mountains, studded with lakes lie north of the A44, just west of Llywernog Silver Lead Mine. It forms the setting for a superb walk (see also unwaymarked walk listed below from same reference point).

Nant-yr-arian, 2½ miles west of Ponterwyd on A44, 8½ miles E. of Aberystwyth. Map sheet 135, reference 718813. Start from Visitor Centre.

(a) Jan.–Dec. 2 ml. 2 hrs. free.
(b) Jan.–Dec. 2½ ml. 2½ hrs. free.

Forestry Commission.

'Bwlch Nant-yr-arian Forest Trail', 10p. and brochure is also available on the Jubilee Walk.

250

Ponterwyd, Dyfed
Bwlch Nant-yr-arian Forest Visitor Centre Rheidol Forest

🅿 5

The new centre, situated on a col has spectacular views over forest and farmland in the foothills of Plynlimon mountain mass.

The centre's exhibition takes its major theme from man's influence in fashioning the landscape, traces a history of the forest and gives an insight into the life and work of a forester in Rheidol forest today.

At Nant-yr-arian, on A44, 9 miles east of Aberystwyth, just

west of Ponterwyd. Map sheet 135, reference 718813.

Opening times:
Easter – September
Sun.–Fri. 10.00am–5.00pm
Sat. 12.30am–5.00pm

July and August – Remains open till 7.00 pm.

Forestry Commission.

Small admission charge.

251

Pontrhydygroes, Dyfed
Tynbedw Forest Walk

🅿 A 5

A waymarked 2 mile walk showing life and growth in the Ystwyth Forest and gorge scenery.

10 miles S.E. of Aberystwyth, off by-road linking B4340 and Pontrhydygroes. Map sheet 135, reference 694716.

Jan.–Dec. 2 miles 1½ hours free.

Forestry Commission.

Waymarked only.

252

Trawsgoed, Dyfed
Black Covert Forest Walk and Coed Allt Fedw, Butterfly Reserve

🅿 A 5

In the middle reaches of Afon Ystwyth, lies Trawsgoed, or Crosswood, a house of the gentry, now an agricultural college. Nearby Black Covert provides a walk in pleasantly hilly, forested landscape.

Trawsgoed, 3 miles S.E. of Llanilar on A485 coast road south of Aberystwyth. Map sheet 135, reference 668728. Start at picnic site by the river.

Jan.–Dec. 1 mile 1 hour free

Forestry Commission and West Wales Naturalists' Trust.

Guide available, 17p.

253

Tre'r Ddol, Dyfed
Pant Glas Forest Walks

🅿 A 5

Series of 3 waymarked walks in forest setting.

7 miles N. of Aberystwyth, off A487. Map sheet 135, reference 568933.

Jan.-Dec.

Walk 1:	½ mile	¾ hour	free.
Walk 2:	¾ mile	1¼ hours	free.
Walk 3:	1¼ miles	2 hours	free.

Forestry Commission.
Waymarked only.

254

| Aberdyfi | 640986 | 6 |

P B 3 6

Happy Valley road at 640986, E. to Llyn Barfog, S. to Carn March Arthur, W.S.W. for 3 miles to Bwlchgwyn E.N.E. above Afon Dyffryn Gwyn to start.

255

| Borth | 624880 | 4-8 |

P A 3 5

Dolybont, up the Leri for about miles (to taste), first by S. bank, then N. bank and back.

256

| Clarach, nr. Aberystwyth | 586841 | 4 |

P A 6

Glan-y-mor S. to Constitution Hill, back by Ty-hen, 590833, then E. and N. to Allt-glais, tracks and paths to start.

257

| Clarach, nr. Aberystwyth | 586841 | 7 |

P B 1

Glan-y-mor N. to Borth and back by the cliffs.

258

| Commins Coch | 846032 | 11 |

C 6

W. over Cefn Coch, via Standing Stone 3½ miles, to Abercegir-Abergwydol road at 81026, E. and N.E. to Cemaes Road, Pont Doldwymyn, E. to Cnllwyn, S.E. to Bryn-moel and back to start.

259

| Devil's Bridge | 753792 | 5 |

P B 5 6

Ysbyty-Cynfyn, Parson's Bridge, W. and W.S.W. to road at 738788, follow S.S.E. and N.E. to 743783, path N.N.E. to Parson's Bridge and back.

260

| Dolgoch, nr. Tywyn | 649047 | 1½ |

P A 3 5

Dolgoch station of Talyllyn Narrow Gauge Railway to Dolgoch Waterfalls, Nant Dolgoch and return.

261

| Hengwm Valley, Machynlleth | 793959 | 6 |

P B 3 6

Afon Hengwm Valley (off Afon Dulas, 6 miles S.E. of Machynlleth) from 793959, cross Afon Hengwm and follow W. side to see the waterfall and basin. Return same way.

262

| Llanddeiniol, nr. Aberystwyth | 561721 | 6 |

P B 6

Llanddeiniol, Pencwm Mawr, Tynbwlch, Mynachdy'r-graig (557747), then S. and E. to Berth-Rhys and back.

263

| Llanddeiniol, nr. Aberystwyth | 569752 | 5 |

P B 1 6

From ½ mile S.W. of Blaenplwyf to Ffoslas, Llety'r gegin (568767), Ty'n-y-fron (573770) and back by minor road or continue along coast from 567772 to Aberystwyth and bus back.

264

| Llyfnant Valley, Machynlleth | 758963 | 6 |

P B 6

From Cwm-cemrhiw, S.E. via Rhiw Goch to peak at 760940, track down past Pistyll y Llyn to start.

265

| Machynlleth | 708975 | 13 |

P C 3 5

From 1 mile N.E. of Glandyfi, up the road on S. side of Llyfnant Valley, Glaspwll, S. to Llechwedd-Einion, and 733941, then W. and N.W. to 706950 then N. to Dynyn and back.

266

| Pennant, nr. Staylittle | 863940 | 6 |

P B 6

S. and S.W. from Pennant at 874967 to near Inn at Dylife, E. to beyond Ffrwd Fawr (878940) then N. to Pennant.

267

| Ponterwyd | 718813 | 6 |

P B 5 6

From 2 miles W. of Ponterwyd, follow the leat N. to road, then E. to 723834. S. back over Esgair Gorlan, then by R.U.P.P. S.S.W. to start.

268

| Pontrhydygroes | 734729 | 10 |

P C 5 6

Pontrhydygroes S. and W. through Maen-Arthur Wood to 687718 back over Cefn Blewog Camp, and alternative routes to Maen Arthur.

Map 136
Newtown
and Llanidloes

Newtown and Llanidloes

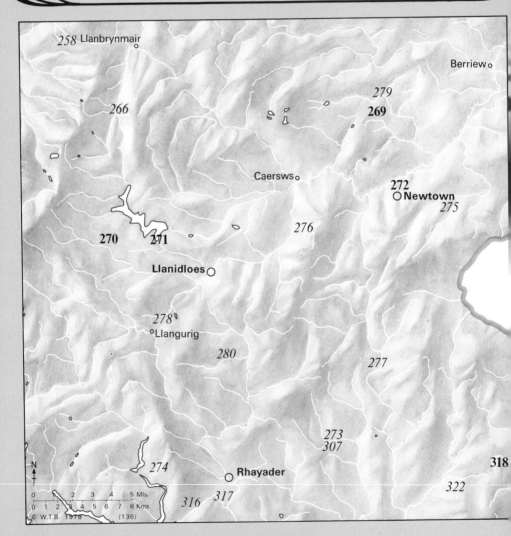

258 Llanbrynmair

Berriew

266

279

269

Caersws

272
Newtown
275

270 271

276

Llanidloes

278
Llangurig

280

277

273
307

N

274

318

Rhayader

322

0   2   3   4   5 Mls.
0 1 2 3 4 5 6 7 8 Kms.
© W.T.B. 1978   (136)

316   317

48

269

Gregynog, near Newtown, Powys
Gregynog Nature Trail

P A 5

The grounds of Gregynog Hall, part of the University of Wales, lie north of Newtown and were formerly the home of the Misses Gwendoline and Margaret Davies. This small woodland trail is notable for its bird life.

Gregynog, 5 miles north of Newtown on minor road. Map sheet 136, reference 085976.

Jan.–Dec.   ½ mile   20 mins.   free

University of Wales, Gregynog Hall, in conjunction with North Wales Naturalists' Trust.

A new brochure is being prepared, small charge.

270

Llanidloes, Powys
Hafren Forest Walks

P A 3 5 6

1. Cascades Forest Trail
A walk along the bank of the headwaters of the River Severn and through Hafren Forest.
Jan.–Dec.   1 mile   ¾ hour   free.

2. Hafren Falls Walk
An energetic walk to Hafren Waterfall on the headwaters of the River Severn.
Jan.–Dec.   3¾ miles   1½ hours free.

3. Hore-Tanllwyth Walk
Walk alongside streams and through Hafren Forest in the Cambrian mountains.
Jan.–Dec.   3¾ miles   1½ hours free.

4. Maesnant Walk
A 3 mile walk through Hafren Forest.
Jan.–Dec.   3 miles   1¼ hours free.

5. Severn-Nant Ricket Walk
A 3½ mile walk through Hafren Forest and alongside the River Severn.
Jan.–Dec.   3½ miles   2½ hours free.

6. Severn-Plynlimon-Garreg Wen Walk
Strenuous walk alongside streams, rivers and through Hafren Forest.
Jan.–Dec.   8 miles   4 hours free.

All walks 7 miles W. of Llanidloes on Old Hall road. Map sheet 136, reference 857869.

Forestry Commission.

'Hafren Forest Walks', 30p.

'Cascades Forest Trail', 5p.

271

Llanidloes, Powys
Llyn Clywedog Scenic Trail

P A 3 5

A pleasant 2½ mile circuit through wooded dingle on hills sloping towards reservoir shore.

On S. shore of Clywedog Reservoir, off B4518, W. of Llanidloes. Map sheet 136, reference 904873. Parking for cars and coaches at reference 915888 off B4518 and also S. of the dam.

Jan.–Dec.   2½ miles   1½ hours free.

Clywedog Reservoir Joint Authority.

'Llyn Clywedog Scenic Trail', small charge, available at local Tourist Information Centre (see back of book).

272

Newtown, Powys
Town Trail No. 1

P 🚻 ♿ 7

Its past as an agricultural centre and most important weaving centre of Wales gives the town a fascinating mixture of roles and styles of buildings, brought out in this trail.

Newtown on A483 Welshpool to Llandrindod Wells road. Map sheet 136, reference 1192.

Jan.–Dec.   1¾ miles   1 hour free.

Newtown Civic Society.

Leaflet available locally.

273

Abbey Cwmhir	057712	8

P B 4 6

Lane behind Hall, N.E. nearly to Porth (at 065736), S.W. to Cwmysgawen Common and road at 024707, S.E. to Cairn, short of second Cairn, N.N.E. to start.

274

Elan Valleys, Rhayader	916674	7

P B 3 6

Pen-y-garreg Bridge up to bridleway, W. then N.E. around Crugyn Gwyddel to road at 933698, W. 2½ miles past Roman Camp by R.U.P.P. to Craig Goch dam, S.E. along reservoir to start.

275

Kerry, nr. Newtown	149863	8

P B 6

From 149863 on Kerry Hill, W.S.W. 2 miles to Two Tumps at 118851, S.E. round Cilfaesty Hill to Panty Hill, to 159837 near Rhuddw Brook, N. and N.W. from beyond Oak Farm to start.

276

Llandinam	025883	6

P B 6

Llandinam, E.S.E. to Cobbler's Gate, N.N.E. to Little London and back, either same route or S.E. to W.T. Mast or E. to Cobbler's Gate

277

Llanbadarn Fynydd	060786	5

P B 4 6

David's Well, N.W. and S. to Fowler's Arm Chair S. and E. to road and back.

278

Llangurig	908792	11

P C 6

Track S.W. 4 miles over Cistfaen to road, which follow S.E. to Bodtalog and take track N.N.E. to Pantgwyn Hill and back to start.

279

Tregynon, nr. Newtown	069957	6

P B 4 6

Bwlch-y-Ffridd, N.E. to Skew Bridge at 088982, S.E. then S.W. to start via 083962.

280

Tylwch, nr. Llanidloes	975787	7

P B 6

From 1 mile S. of Tylwch, walk W. then S. to Standing Stone (955772), back by Alltlwyd.

Map 137
Ludlow and
Wenlock Edge

Montgomery and New Radnor

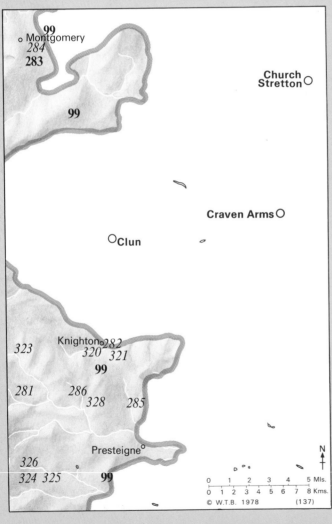

99
o Montgomery
284
283

99

Church
Stretton O

Craven Arms O

O Clun

Knighton o *282*
323   *320* *321*
99

281   *286*
328   *285*

Presteigne °

326
324 *325*   **99**

N
↑

| 0 | 1 | 2 | 3 | 4 | 5 Mls. |

| 0 | 1 | 2 | 3 | 4 | 5 | 6 | 7 | 8 Kms. |

© W.T.B. 1978   (137)

281

| Bleddfa | 206684 | 5 |

🅿 B 6

N.W. to St. Michael's Pool, N.E. and E. to Pitch Hill and back to start.

282

| Knighton | 292720 | 6 |

🅿 ⬛ B 6

Lane S.S.E. path into and up Cwm, Mount Flirt, E. to lane, S.S.E. to cross-roads, Llan-wen Hill, join Offa's Dyke Path at 279698 to return to Knighton.

283

Montgomery, Powys
A walk around Montgomery

🅿 A 7

Montgomery is a mediaeval 'new town' founded in the 1220's at the foot of a precipitous rock outcrop where Henry III built a castle, part of the border defences against the Welsh.

The town is important historically because the mediaeval street layout remains virtually unchanged, and architecturally because it is a fine example of an almost unspoilt small Georgian market town.

Montgomery, 7 miles north-east of Newtown, Map sheet 137. Jan.–Dec. 1 mile 1 hour free

Montgomery Civic Society and Town Council.

'A Walk around Montgomery', small charge, available locally.

284

| Montgomery | 223965 | 9 |

P B 4 6

To castle above town, left to Town Hill Monument and S. on path to quarry lane. Left and reach road at phone box (218944). E. and then S. up small lane, going S. In a mile, past ravine, path E. to pass New House to A489 (225927). E. for ½ mile; past national boundary turn right on path which crosses stream into lane running E. At B4385, by Mellington Hall gates, turn N. along Offa's Dyke Path for 2 miles to 241961, path crosses from left to right side of dyke at estate road; turn left past Lymore to Montgomery (ODA).

285

| Norton, nr. Presteigne | 304673 | 4 |

P B 6

Norton, W. and N.W. by various alternatives including Offa's Dyke Path, to Monument Hill at 285688, E. to Hill House Farm, S.W. and S. to start.

WTB © 1978

286

| Pilleth, nr. Presteigne | 257680 | 3–7 |

P B 6

See Pilleth Church, N.W. to Black Hill and return by track down Cwm or continue via Hendregenny, W. to Beacons, S. to Monaughty, return by tracks S. of River Lugg.

Woodlands, forests and shady places.

Oak

Birch

Green Woodpecker

Scots Pine

Grey Squirrel

Sitka Spruce

Ivy

Fox-Glove

Ring Dove

Bramble

Badger

Chick

Woodcock

Oak leaves

Primrose

Map 145
Cardigan

Cardigan

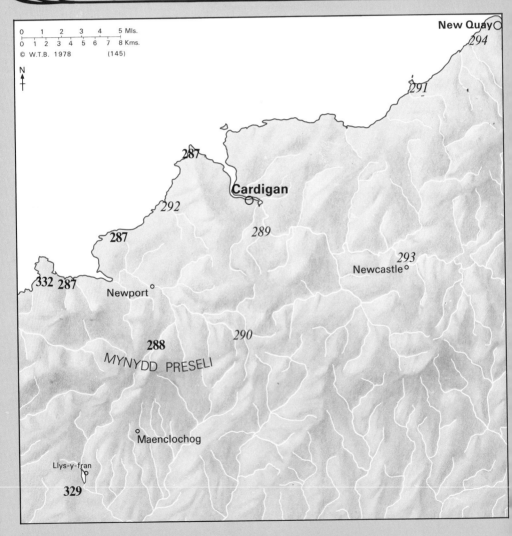

0   1   2   3   4   5 Mls.
0   1   2   3   4   5   6   7   8 Kms.
© W.T.B. 1978   (145)

N

New Quay○
294

291

287

Cardigan
○

292

287   *289*

293
Newcastle ○

332 **287**

Newport ○

288   *290*

MYNYDD PRESELI

○ Maenclochog

Llys-y-fran
○
329

52

Pembrokeshire Coast Path,
Dyfed

P ⬚ ⊕ A B C 1

167 miles Long Distance Footpath, mainly along the cliff-tops in Pembrokeshire Coast National Park. Magnificent stretches of cliffs alternating with rocky coves and sandy bays. Rich sea bird population and a profusion of coastal flowers and plants at the appropriate times of the year.

From a point 2 miles N.W. of St. Dogmael's (Map sheet 145, reference 153485) near Cardigan, to Amroth (Map sheet 158, reference 163071) near Saunders-foot, by way of Fishguard, St. David's, Milford Haven, Angle, Manorbier and Tenby.

Jan.–Dec. Join or leave at free many points around coast

Pembrokeshire Coast National Park Authority and Countryside Commission.

'The Pembrokeshire Coast Path', by John Barrett, H.M.S.O., £2.50. 'Walking the Pembroke-shire Coast Path', by Patrick Stark, 50p, and 'Pembrokeshire Coast Path', by Tony Roberts, are widely available in local bookshops.

Restrictions: Most of the Coast Path is 'open' at all times. However, certain sections in the neighbourhood of the Castle-martin Ranges, S. of Pembroke, are closed when the Army is firing. Details from Castlemartin Range (Tel. Castlemartin 321), Information Centres (Easter – October), Bosherston Post Office (Tel. Castlemartin 286) or local newspapers. Keep to the public footpath and take great care along the cliff paths, especially if it is windy.

288

Preseli Mountains, Dyfed
Open Hills and Moorland

P ⊕ B C 6

The Preseli Mountains, most of which are in the Pembrokeshire Coast National Park, are an upland moorland region, reaching

A special bus service links interesting stretches of the Pembrokeshire Coast Path. Enquire at National Park Information Centres listed at the back of this book.

1,760 feet at their highest point. Interesting natural history and archaeological area. There are no waymarked footpaths.

North Pembrokeshire, S. of Newport. Served by the A487 Fishguard to Cardigan road, A40 Fishguard to Haverfordwest road, A478 Cardigan to Tenby road, and crossed by the B4329 Cardigan to Haverfordwest road. Map sheets 145 and 157.

Jan.–Dec. Various free.

Pembrokeshire Coast National Park Authority.

National Park leaflet entitled 'The Preseli Hills', free.

289

Cilgerran	195430	To taste

P A 3 5

Cilgerran along the river in either direction and back.

290

Crymych	165331	4 or 9

P B 6

1¼ miles W. of Crymych to Carnmenyn 144325 and back or continue over Carnbica to 122323 returning N.E. to 145350, then S.E.E. and S. around N. edge of Foeldrygarn to start by R.U.P.P.

291

Llangrannog	311542	5–6

P A 1

Llangrannog (1) N.E. to Ynys Lochtyn (National Trust), Cefn Cwrt, past Felin Uchaf (327542) and back. (2) S.W. to Penbryn and back.

292

Moylegrove	110455	To taste

P A 1

Ceibwr Bay along the Pembrokeshire Coast Path either N. or S.

293

Newcastle Emlyn	295420	3

P A 3

Cwmcoy near Newcastle Emlyn, N.E. along Afon Ceri and back on other side.

294

New Quay	355576	8

P B 1

Cwmtudu to New Quay by coast, back by Ty-rhos and Byrlip or along coast.

Map 146
Lampeter and
Llandovery

Lampeter and Llandovery

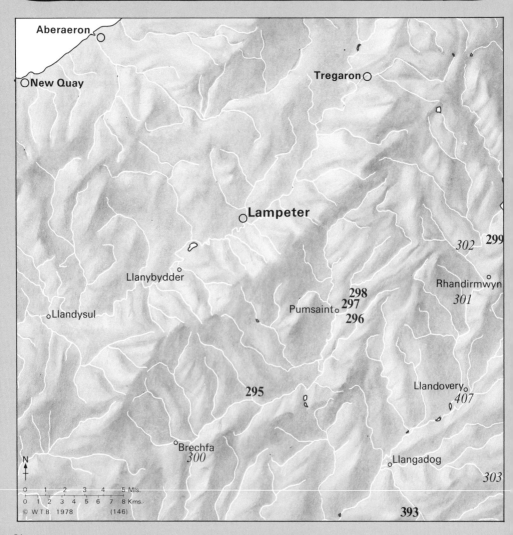

Aberaeron

New Quay

Tregaron

Lampeter

302 **299**

Llanybydder

Rhandirmwyn
301

Llandysul

Pumsaint **298**
297
296

295

Llandovery
407

N

Brechfa
300

Llangadog

303

0 1 2 3 4 5 Mls.
0 1 2 3 4 5 6 7 8 Kms.
© W T B. 1978   (146)

393

295

Abergorlech, Dyfed
Abergorlech Forest Walk,
Brechfa Forest

P A 5

1½ – 2 miles walk in the extensive Brechfa forest which clothes the northern slopes of the beautiful Vale of Cothi.

Abergorlech village, map 146, reference 587336, 8 miles N.W. of Llandeilo. Start at car park in village on B4310, Llansawel to Brechfa road.

Jan.–Dec. 1½–2 miles 1 hour free.

Forestry Commission.

Waymarked.

Abergorlech in the hills near Carmarthen.

296

Caeo, Dyfed
Caeo Forest Walk

P A 5

This waymarked walk explores the forested area in the narrow Annell Valley near Pumsaint, an area mined by the Romans for gold that lie beneath the hills.

Caeo, 1½ miles E. of Pumsaint, off A482 Llanwrtyd Wells to Lampeter road. Map sheet 146, reference 679405. Start on forest road ½ mile N. of Caeo village.

Jan.–Dec. 1 mile 1½ hours free.

Forestry Commission.

Waymarked.

297

Pumsaint, Dyfed
Dolaucothi Nature Trails

P A 5 6 7

Two trails on National Trust land in the wooded Cothi Valley around Pumsaint, scene in Roman times, from the 1st century A.D. and later, of gold mining activity. Aqueduct systems, opencast works and adits, of Roman origin, can be seen.

Pumsaint on A482 Llandovery – Lampeter road, 8 miles N.W. of Llanwrda. Map sheet 146, reference 664404.

Jan.–Dec.		free.
Tour 1	1 mile	1½ hours
Tour 2	½ mile	1 hour

National Trust.

'The Roman Gold Mines at Dolaucothi', (30p plus postage) from Carmarthen County Museum.

298

Pumsaint, Dyfed
Estate Walk

P A 4

A walk through part of 2,577 acre Dolaucothi Estate of the National Trust designed to show some aspects of the management of a large country estate of woodland, lowland and hill farms.

Pumsaint, on A482 Llanwrda – Lampeter road. Map sheet 146, reference 653410.

Jan.–Dec. 1½ miles 1 hour free.

National Trust in conjunction with Forestry Commission and Ministry of Agriculture.

'Estate Walk at Pumsaint', (30p plus postage) from National Trust, 22 Alan Road, Llandeilo SA19 6HU Tel. Llandeilo 3476.

299

Rhandirmwyn, Near
Llandovery, Dyfed
Dinas Nature Trail

P A 5

A 10-stage trail through an oakwood gorge on the Towy river's most beautiful section, with a wide variety of native and migratory birds. The rare red kite flies over the area.

2¼ miles N. of Rhandirmwyn (on road to Llyn Brianne, on a minor road N. from A40 at Llandovery) Map sheet 146, reference 788471.

Jan.–Dec. 2 miles 2–2½ hours free.

Royal Society for the Protection of Birds. Warden resident at the Dinas Nature Reserve. Tel. Rhandirmwyn 228.

Information is displayed in the Information Centre and at points on the trail.

300

Brechfa	536285	6

P B 3 4

From Darren-fawr, 2 miles S.E. of Brechfa, W. side of Cothi, to Clynllydan, 533300, W. to road, S. by road and track to 524276, E. to Rhiwiau and back.

301

Llandovery	761421	3 or 8

P A 3 6

(1) To Craig Ddu waterfall and back
(2) N. through Cwm y Rhaiadr forestry plantation to Troed-y-rhiw-fer (764449) and back same way or along road.

302

Llandovery	764449	8

P B 3 4

From Troed-y-rhiw-fer along W. bank of Tywi past Gallt-y-berau (773461) Rhyd-y-groes. (770474), Pen-y-rhiw-iar and back by old road running due S. via 757458.

303

Llandovery	796263	5

P A 6

From a point 4 miles S.E. of Myddfai N.E. and N.W. to 794282 then W. to 782275, then S.E. to start.

Map 147
Elan Valley and
Builth Wells

Elan Valley and Builth Wells

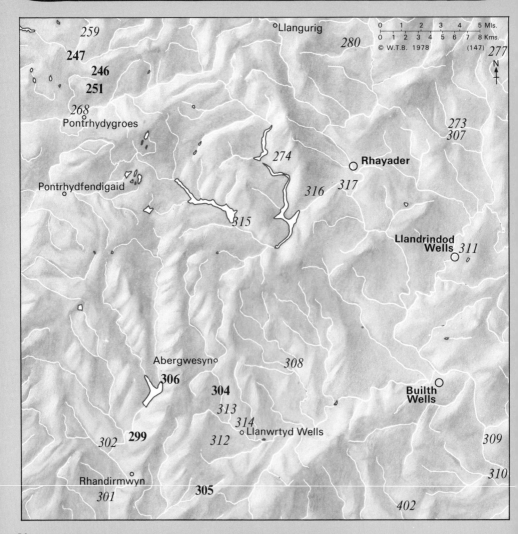

259
Llangurig
280
247
246
251
268
Pontrhydygroes
273
307
274
Rhayader
Pontrhydfendigaid
316
317
315
Llandrindod
Wells 311
Abergwesyn
308
306
304
Builth
Wells
313
299
314
Llanwrtyd Wells
309
302
312
310
Rhandirmwyn
305
301
402

0 1 2 3 4 5 Mls.
0 1 2 3 4 5 6 7 8 Kms.
© W.T.B. 1978 (147)
277
N

304

Abergwesyn, Powys
Cwm Irfon Forest Walks

P   A   5

Short walks in the forests behind Llanwrtyd Wells.

Cwm Irfon, 3 miles N.W. of Llanwrtyd Wells. Map sheet 147, references 856493 and 856507.

Jan.–Dec.   Various   Various   free.

Forestry Commission.

305

Cynghordy, near Llandovery, Dyfed
Sugar Loaf Walk

P   A   6

A walk from the direction board in picnic site on the Sugar loaf mountain to the summit.

Sugar Loaf pass, 4 miles south west of Llanwrtyd Wells on A483 Builth Wells to Llandovery road. Map sheet 147, reference 834428.

Jan.–Dec.   1 mile   1 hour   free.

Dyfed County Council.

Information at picnic site.

306

Rhandirmwyn, Dyfed
Llyn Brianne Walks

P   A   5

Llyn Brianne, a recently constructed reservoir lies deep in the hills north of Llandovery. It is the southern limit of the vast Towy Forest which extends 6 miles north and eastwards to the edge of Abergwesyn.

Llyn Brianne reached by Rhandirmwyn road from Llandovery. Map sheet 147, reference 811507. Start from Car Park.

Jan.–Dec.   Various   –   free.

Forestry Commission.

Not waymarked.

307

Abbeycwmhir	055712	7

P   B   6

Abbeycwmhir, path from left of church then between Y Glog and Little Park N. to 051734 and R.U.P.P. E.N.E. to Porth S.W. back to Cwm Cynnydd bank and down valley to start.

308

Beulah	921512	4–8

P   B   6

From Beulah up track going W. to 888523 and beyond and return or work round by Nant-y-cerdin (873506) and back E. by Aber-Annell.

309

Builth Wells	099454	4–8

P   B   5   6

(1) Llandeilo Graban N.W. to Argoed, and to 086458, then along Llandeilo Hill dropping to starting point when desired. Extend the walk from 086458 via Aberedw Rocks, Llywelyn's Cave back to Llandeilo Hill.

310

Erwood	097430	6

P   B   5   6

From Erwood follow road to Crickadarn and beyond to cross stream and return by paths and tracks.

311

Llandrindod Wells	061609	4 or 7

P   ⧓   ⊕   B   4   6

Woodland path E. side of lake to 065603, Golf Clubhouse. Turn left on road to 073603, fork left, keeping on road to brook, left here through gate to Forestry Commission picnic site at Shaky Bridge (085613). This walk can be extended by walking N.E. from Shaky Bridge, past St. Michael's Church and Cefnllys Castle by lane to Cwm then path N.W. to Alpine Bridge, then direct tracks to 063618, where there is a path S. into town.

312

Llanwrtyd Wells	847443	10

P   ⧓   C   5   6

From 847443 on A483(T) a Forestry Commission track (not on map) runs W.N.W., N.E. and N.W. to 840451, from where take track W. and N. to 840458 then (a) return to start by track going S.W. (2 m), or (b) track N., W. and

S.W. to 822448 where take right branch to track at 818448, then N.E. to 833468 and follow track to Llanwrtyd Old Church and then minor road to A483 and start.

313

Llanwrtyd Wells	865477	6 or 9

P   ⧓   C   5   6

Go N.N.E. from 865477 to Nant-yr-odin, return by (a) 881488, then B.R. to 876475, emerging at 871472 (6 m) or (b) continue to Nant-y-cerdin and Bwlchmawr, then S.S.W. to A483(T) and take B.R. N.W. at 884474 to join route (a).

314

Llanwrtyd Wells	878466	8

P   ⧓   C   6

Llanwrtyd Wells, W.N.W. to Llanwrtyd Church at 864478, Cwm Henog, E. and N. over hill and river to Alltwinau, S.E. to Geneu, Cwm Irfon and back.

315

Rhayader	872634	18

P   C   3   6

Claerwen Dam, W. up Afon Arban, over Carreg-wen Fawr, road S. to 808584, E.N.E. over Drum Nant-y-gorlan and skirting Carreg-llwyd y Rhestr to start.

316

Rhayader	931648	5 or 10

P   B   6

From S. end of suspension bridge in Elan Village, Caban Coch Dam, alongside reservoir to Nant y Gro, S.E. to pick up the track S. around Craig Cnwch to 933635 for track N. to Elan Village. Extend by going to Gro Hill, S.E. to 955611, N.E. to 971631, then bridleway N.W. to road at 958638 which follow to start via Blaencwm and Talwrn or go to Llanwrthwl to pick up bridleway via Cefn and so back.

317

Rhayader	965656	4

P   A   6

Glyn Bridge, 2 miles S. of Rhayader, Bwlch-coch, Glan-rhos (972641), return along road.

Map 148
Presteigne and
Hay on Wye

Presteigne and Hay on Wye

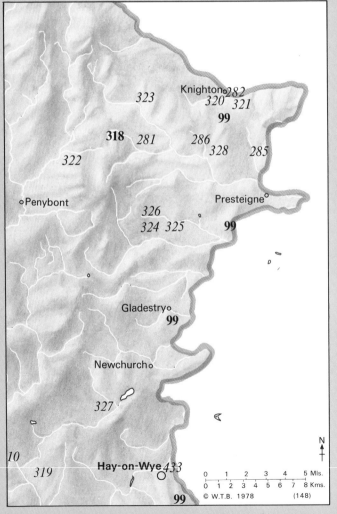

Knighton 282
323   320 321
99
318   281   286
328   285
322
Presteigne
o Penybont
326
324 325   99
Gladestry o
99
Newchurch o
327
10
319
Hay-on-Wye 433
99

0 1 2 3 4 5 Mls.
0 1 2 3 4 5 6 7 8 Kms.
© W.T.B. 1978   (148)

N
↑

318

Bleddfa, Powys
Radnorshire Nature Trail No. 1

P B 5 6

A pleasant 8 mile trail through forestry plantation and trees.

At sign F.R.P.7, Bleddfa Forest on A488, Map sheet 148, reference 189683.

Jan.–Dec. 8 miles (app.) 4–5 hours

Forestry Commission and Mr. Carl D. Ehrenzeller, St. Christopher's Youth Hostel, Ithan Road, Llandrindod Wells, Powys. Tel. 2474.

'Radnorshire (Bleddfa) Nature Trail No. 1'. Available from Mr. M. B. Smith, The Book Shop, Llandrindod Wells, Powys.

319

Builth Wells	114415	7

P B 6

Llanstephan Bridge (9 miles S.E. of Builth Wells), N.W. then N. to Craig Pwlldu, Pwllperran (129441) from where return by tracks and paths S. to start.

320

Knighton	209785	9

P B 6

Dutlas, Beacon Hill, N. to Fair Well (171778) N.E. to Cwm Bugail (180792) E. to Pantycaregle S.W. to Cwmyringel, S. to Fron Rocks and back.

321

Knighton	285725	9

🅿 ⇄ B 4 6

West Street, Offa's Dyke Information Centre, park and path N.W. for 3 miles to 267767 surfaced lane. Left for 1 mile, forward and over ridge to Monaughty Poeth. Over Teme, path right, over B4355 and round W. of Knucklas Castle (easy climb to top). Lane under viaduct and up steep road going S. At 'T' junction on ridge turn E. by small road over old racecourse. Before this descends to B4355 take 270730 path alongside of Garth Hill into Knighton (O.D.A.).

322

Llanfihangel Rhydithon	151667	7

🅿 B 6

Road then track S.E. of church 2½ miles to 165636 from where follow bridleways E. and N.E. round The Riggles at 184654 to near Rhiw Pool, then N.W. and S.W. to Old Hall to lane and back.

323

Llangunllo	207737	6 or 7

🅿 B 4 6

From Llancoch (207737) N.W. to Beacon Lodge (direct or via Ferley), Beacon Hill, E.S.E. to The Farm, S.E. to Heath and back.

324

New Radnor	194592	3

🅿 A 5 6

1 mile N.E. of Llanfihangel Nant Melan to Water-break-its-neck and back to start.

325

New Radnor	212610	7

🅿 B 6

Past site of castle, N. then N.W. side of Forestry skirting Whimble hill, continue by end of Whinyard Rocks to stream head, then along forestry fence E. to 224640, S.W. round head of valley, E. to Ferndale, S.W. by Knowle Hill to start.

326

New Radnor	216616	Various

🅿 A 5 6

New Radnor various walks round and on The Smatcher, 1 mile S. of New Radnor.

327

Painscastle	163440	7

🅿 B 4

From unfenced road S. of Painscastle to the roundabout (155444) from W. side take tracks to near Llanbach Howey (138456) E. to Cwm and Pentre and back.

328

Whitton	273673	7

🅿 B 4 7

Whitton S.W. to Bridge End, N.W. then N. past Castell Foelallt to Pilleth Church. Take metalled track E. curving north to 262691 for track over Rhos Hill to Offa's Dyke at Rhos-y-meirch (279697). Follow this S. 2 miles to 285674, then W., descending to Whitton, keeping farm to left. (O.D.A.).

Offas Dyke Countryside Path runs from Prestatyn to Chepstow, 167 miles. The Dyke was the work of King Offa of Mercia between AD 757 and 796 as a defence against his Welsh neighbours.

Map 157
St. David's and
Haverfordwest

St. David's and Haverfordwest

338   287   332 287

Fishguard ○

287

287

287
340

St David's ○ 287   341 342

287   344   Llys-y-fran ○
336   329

287

339
333

Broad Haven   ○ Haverfordwest

287

335

334   Milford
○ Haven

287

331
Dale ○

287   Pembroke ○ 330
Dock
337   Pembroke
287   ○ 347

N

0   1   2   3   4   5 Mls.
0   1   2   3   4   5   6   7   8 Kms.
© W.T.B. 1978   (157)

60

Clarbeston, near

Haverfordwest, Dyfed
*Llysyfran Reservoir Country Park
Walks*

🅿 A 3 4 5

The Country Park at Llysyfran Reservoir has plenty to interest the family walker. Facilities provided at the reservoir include car parks, toilet block, a wardening service, a slipway, a boat park and picnic sites, also a small cafe.

A footpath has been provided around the edge of the reservoir. The variety of plant and animal life at Llys-y-Fran, on land as well as in the water, makes a walk along this perimeter path an extremely rewarding one for all interested in natural history.

Llysyfran Reservoir, 8 miles N.E. of Haverfordwest and 3 miles N. of Clarbeston Road village. Map sheet 157, reference 040244.

Jan.–Dec. 7½ miles 2½ hours free.

Dyfed County Council and Welsh Water Authority.

'Llysyfran Reservoir Country Park', 2p.

A Nature Trail is currently being formulated and a brochure will be published when it is complete.

330

Cosheston, near Pembroke,
Dyfed
Upton Castle Grounds – Walks

🅿 A 5

Upton lies within the Daugleddau section of the Pembrokeshire Coast National Park which is centred upon the inner tidal reaches of Milford Haven. An all-weather footpath leads from the car park and connects the Dell with the formal Terraces; elsewhere the paths, although clearly waymarked, are less formal. The grounds, which contain over 250 different species of trees and shrubs, are at their best in spring, although the flowering season commences in December and continues through until early summer.

3 miles east of Pembroke Dock and 1 mile north of A477 Carmarthen to Pembroke Dock

road. Approach through Cosheston Village. Map sheet 157, reference 020046.

Feb.–Oct., inclusive, Various free. 10.00 a.m.–4.30 p.m. walks Tues., Weds., Thurs., Fris. and Spring and Summer Bank Holiday Mondays

Castle owners and Pembrokeshire Coast National Park Authority. Warden on site.

'Upton Castle Grounds', 10p.

331

Dale, Pembrokeshire, Dyfed
Dale Peninsula Path

🅿 B 1 2

A walk around the Dale Peninsula and St. Ann's Head, along part of the Pembrokeshire Coast Path – one of the Countryside Commission's Long Distance Footpaths. An accompanying booklet looks particularly at the geology and scenery of the peninsula, and its history from prehistoric times up to the present.

Dale, 13 miles S.W. of Haverfordwest on B4327, Map sheet 157, reference 812056.

Jan.–Dec. 7 miles 4–5 hours free.

'A Plain Man's Guide to the Path around the Dale Peninsula', by John Barrett, 25p, available locally and from Pembrokeshire Coast National Park Authority.

332

Fishguard, Pembrokeshire
Dyfed
Dinas Island Walk

🅿 ⊕ B 1

In the Pembrokeshire Coast National Park. Circuit of Dinas 'Island' along part of Pembrokeshire Coastal Path, the long distance footpath established by the Countryside Commission. Dinas 'Island' is really a headland, linked to the mainland by a narrow valley. The walk follows the cliff path – in parts quite steep – and climbs to nearly 500 feet at Dinas Head.

4 miles E. of Fishguard off the A487 at Dinas. Map sheet 157, reference 015401.

Jan.–Dec. 3 miles 3 hours free.

West Wales Naturalists' Trust.

'Dinas Island – a Brief Natural History Guide', 12p.

333

Haverfordwest, Dyfed
Walks in Withybush Woods

🅿 ⊕ A 5

Waymarked and signposted walks on public footpaths through woodlands lying east of Withybush Airfield, 2 miles north of the town.

Withybush Woods, on a side road right from A40 junction, one mile north of Haverfordwest town centre. Map 157, reference 963188.

Jan.–Dec. Various free.

Dyfed County Council.

334

Marloes, Haverfordwest, Dyfed
Marloes Sands Nature Trail

🅿 A 1

The trail explores the Silurian and Old Red Sandstone cliffs, with spectacular coastal scenery, returning past an Iron Age fort and the flat expanse of Marloes Mere with its reeds and cotton grass. Ravens and choughs may be seen as well as grey seals along the coast. For the most part the trail follows part of the Pembrokeshire Coast Path, the Long Distance Footpath established by the Countryside Commission.

Marloes Sands, 13 miles S.W. of Haverfordwest reached by a minor road leaving B4327, 2 miles N. of Dale. Map sheet 157.

Jan.–Dec. 1½ miles 1 hour free.

West Wales Naturalists' Trust.

'Marloes Nature Trail' 17p.

335

Skomer, Pembrokeshire Coast, Dyfed
Skomer Island Nature Trail

🅿 A 1

Skomer Island is a National Nature Reserve, owned by the Nature Conservancy Council and managed by the

West Wales Naturalists' Trust. It is noted for its sea bird colonies. There are two routes around the island.

1 mile from the mainland off the Pembrokeshire Coast, near Marloes 13 miles S.W. of Haverfordwest. Map sheet 157. Embarkation point is Martin's Haven, Map sheet 157, reference 761091.

West Wales Naturalists' Trust. Resident Warden or his assistant meets boats landing. A charge is made for the boat as well as a small landing fee.

'Skomer Island'. 15p from National Park Information Centres (Easter–October) or 35p by post from the West Wales Naturalists' Trust.

336

Treffgarne, Dyfed
Nant-y-Coy Nature Walk

🅿 A 1 6

Nant-y-Coy grounds are privately owned and include Great Treffgarne Rocks, one of the most prominent physical features for miles around. The walk gives birdseye views of the gorge in which the mill sits.

Treffgarne on A40, 7 miles north of Haverfordwest on the Fishguard road. Map sheet 157, reference 956252. Start at Nant-y-Coy Mill Shop.

Jan.–Dec.   2 miles   2 hours   free.

Wilson's of Nant-y-Coy Mill, Treffgarne.
Pamphlet available.
See also walk from point 956252.

337

Angle	865029	4

🅿 A 1

From Angle round North Hill via Angle Point and Chapel Bay.

338

Fishguard	893385	4

🅿 A 1

Pwllderi car park, along coast path to Strumble Head, S. to Tresinwen, Garnfechan, overslopes of Garn-fawr and back.

339

Haverfordwest	956252	5

🅿 A 1 6

Treffgarne Camp and Maiden Castle, Poll Carn, Great Treffgarne mountain and back. (See also Nant-y-Coy Nature Walk).

340

St. David's	723272	4–7

🅿 A 1

From Whitesand Bay N.W. to St. David's Head on Coast Path and back round Carnllidi or Carn Treliwyd.

Herring Gull

Manx Shearwater

Cormorant

Cormorant

Shag

Centaury

Marjor

Cliffs and sunny screes.

Herring Gull

Gannet

Fulmar

Gannet

Gannet

Guillemot

Razorbill

Immature Black-Backed Gull

Puffin

Tree Mallow

Sea Pink

Musk Mallow

Centaury

341

Solva	800240	7

🅿 ⊕ **B 1**

Solva W. along Pembrokeshire Coast path to St. Non's Well (752243) and St. David's (Part National Trust). Bus back.

342

Solva	816245	4

🅿 ⊕ **A 1**

Walk from ¾ mile E. of Solva to Dinas-fawr, via Burial Chamber W. to Penrhyn, Gribin and back. (Part National Trust).

Map 158
Tenby

Tenby

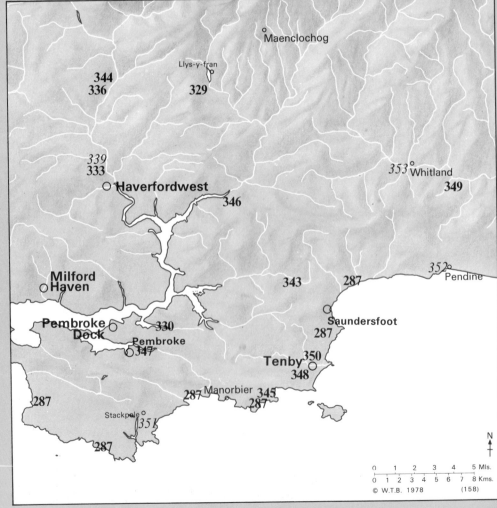

Maenclochog

Llys-y-fran

344
336

329

339
333

○ **Haverfordwest**

346

353 ○ Whitland

349

**Milford
Haven**

343   287

352 ○ Pendine

**Pembroke
Dock**

330

287 ○ Saundersfoot

287

Pembroke
○ 347

350
Tenby ○
348

287   Manorbier   345
287

Stackpole ○
351

287

287

N

| 0 | 1 | 2 | 3 | 4 | 5 Mls. |

| 0 | 1 | 2 | 3 | 4 | 5 | 6 | 7 | 8 Kms. |

© W.T.B. 1978   (158)

343

Kilgetty, Dyfed
A Short Walk in the Pembrokeshire Coalfield

🅿 A 4 7

A waymarked walk in the rural surroundings of the Kilgetty Tourist Information Centre of Pembrokeshire Coast National Park. Underfoot are the remains of one of the earliest coalfields that made Saundersfoot a larger coal port than Cardiff in the early 19th century.

Kilgetty at the crossroads of A477, St. Clears to Pembroke Dock and A478 Narberth to Tenby roads. Map sheet 158, reference 122072.

Jan.–Dec. 2½ miles 1½–2 hrs. free.

Pembrokeshire Coast National Park Authority.

'A Walk in the Pembrokeshire Coalfield', 6p.

344 *(See also 329.)*

Llysyfran, Dyfed
Llysyfran Reservoir Country Park

🅿 A 3 4 5

The recently created reservoir of Llys-y-fran in a wooded valley in the foothills of the Preseli Mountains offers views, fishing, boating and a nature trail.

Llys-y-fran, a village 8 miles N.E. of Haverfordwest. Map sheet 158, reference 035243.

Jan.–Dec. Various walks free. from Picnic Site

Dyfed County Council, Countryside Commission and Welsh Water Authority.

345

Lydstep, South Pembrokeshire, Dyfed
Lydstep Headland Nature Trail

A 1

A headland walk, along part of the Pembrokeshire Coastal Path, the Long Distance Footpath established by the Countryside Commission, partly on National Trust property.

½ mile S. of Lydstep, a village on A4139, 3½ miles W. of Tenby. Map sheet 158, reference 077978.

Jan.–Dec. 1½ miles 1 hour free. West Wales Naturalists' Trust.

'Lydstep Headland Nature Trail', 17p.

346

Narberth, Pembrokeshire, Dyfed
Slebech Forest Trail

🅿 A 5

A forest walk through Forestry Commission property overlooking the Eastern Cleddau river.

Minwear Wood, Slebech Forest on minor road to Minwear, 1½ miles S.W. of A40 and A4075 junction at Canaston Bridge. 3 miles W. of Narberth. Map sheet 158, reference 056139.

Easter to 1 mile 1 hour free. 30th Sept.

Forestry Commission.

'A walk in Slebech Forest', 5p.

347

Pembroke, Dyfed
A Walk around Pembroke

🅿 ⇄ ⊕ A 7

Centrepiece of this walk around the ancient town of Pembroke is the mighty Castle first established in 1090 by the Normans. The long Main Street is the scene in autumn of the long established Pembroke Fair.

Pembroke. Map sheet 158, reference 982616.

Jan.–Dec. 2 miles 1½ hours free. (Charge to Castle)

South Pembrokeshire District Council.

'A Walk around Pembroke', brochure, small charge.

Pembroke is an old town, dominated by an 11th – 12th century castle.

Penally, South Pembrokeshire, Dyfed
Penally Nature Trail

P ⇄ ⊕ **B** 4

A trail starting and finishing at Penally village, which uses by-roads and paths in and around the ancient Ridgeway route to Pembroke.

Penally on A4139, 2 miles S.W. of Tenby, map sheet 158. Start Crown Inn, Penally, reference 117991.

Jan.–Dec. 3½ miles 3 hours free.

Friends of Penally, 'Penally Nature Trail', 5p, available locally.

349

St. Clears, Dyfed
Redgate Forest Walk

P A 5

A short and easy walk that explores a wooded valley 1 mile up Afon Taf.

Llanddowror, 2 miles west of St. Clears, on A477 St. Clears to Pembroke Dock road, map sheet 158, reference 235142. Start 1¼ miles along on minor road between Llanddowror and Tavernspite.

Jan.–Dec. 1 mile 1½ hours free.

Forestry Commission.
Waymarked.

350

Tenby, South Pembrokeshire, Dyfed
Rambles around Tenby

P A 1 4

A selection of cliff, coastal and country walks in and near the Pembrokeshire Coast National Park in the area around Tenby.

Tenby, map sheet 158.

Tenby is directly on the Pembrokeshire Coast Path. An interesting diversion takes the walker to Caldey Island (see below).

Name	Miles	Hrs.
Cliff Walks:		
Waterwynch	4	2
Waterwynch ⎫	4½	2
Monkstone ⎬	(one way)	
Saundersfoot ⎭		
Giltar Point	3	1½
Giltar Point ⎫	3½	2
Proud Giltar ⎬	(one way)	
Lydstep Head ⎬	4½	3
Lydstep Caverns ⎭	(one way)	

Country Walks:		
Causeway Mill ⎫		
Ford Green ⎬	4½	2
Gumfreston ⎭		
Scotsborough Ruins ⎫		
and Wood ⎬	4	2¼
Folly Lane ⎬		
Wester Lane ⎭		
Black Rock ⎫		
Hoyles Mouth Cave ⎬	5	3
Ridgeway ⎬		
Penally ⎭		
(Torch needed if visiting cave)		
Black Rock ⎫		
Causeway ⎬	4	2
Nabbs Bridge ⎭		
Island Walk:		
Caldey Island	2	2
(plus crossing time).		

South Pembrokeshire District Council

'Rambles around Tenby', 5p.

351

Pembroke	993957	9

P B 1 2 3

Stackpool Quay to Barafundle Bay, Broad Haven and Bosherton Ponds and back.

352

Pendine	233079	7–9

P 1 4

Pendine along the coast W. to Amroth or up to Marros and back down the valley to the start

353

Whitland	201159	4

P ⇄ ⊕ A 4

Whitland (Tre-Vaughan), S. to Cyffic, E. along road to 225138, N. to Great Pale and back.

Map 159
Swansea and Gower

Swansea and Gower

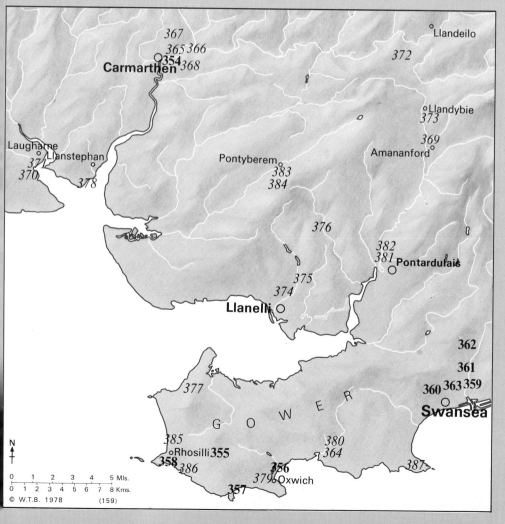

367
365 366
354
368
Carmarthen

Llandeilo

372

Llandybie
373

369
Amananford

Laugharne
371
370
Llanstephan
378

Pontyberem
383
384

376

382
381
Pontardulais

375
374

Llanelli

362

361

360 363 359

Swansea

377

G O W E R

385
Rhosilli 355
358
386

380
364

356
379 Oxwich

387

357

N

0   1   2   3   4   5 Mls.
0 1 2 3 4 5 6 7 8 Kms.

© W.T.B. 1978   (159)

Carmarthen, Dyfed
Exploring Carmarthen on foot

P ⇄ ⊕ A 7

Overlooking the Towy river, 12 miles from the sea, Carmarthen the administrative capital of Dyfed is a commercial and agricultural centre of great historic interest. Features range from coracles on the river, a roman amphitheatre, castle remains and market.

Carmarthen on A40, A48. Map sheet 159, reference 4120.

Jan.–Dec.

Eastern Trail 1½ mls. 1½ hrs. free.

Western Trail 1 ml 1 hr. free.

Carmarthen Civic Society.

'Exploring Carmarthen on foot', available locally, small charge.

Interwined laths of willow and hazel go to make up the basic frame of the coracle which is based on patterns which have scarcely changed since the Iron Age. Long before the Romans came to Britain in the 1st century A.D. these boats, as light as thistledown, would be seen drifting on the rivers of West Wales and elsewhere in Britain. Today they are confined almost exclusively to the rivers Teifi and Tywi and particularly to that stretch around Cenarth and Cilgerran on the Teifi, and Carmarthen town on the Tywi. Conditions on the two rivers call for slightly different craft. Those of the Teifi face turbulent eddies and lie much deeper in the water. That of the Tywi skims much more lightly over the placid waters. A noticeable difference is in the shape viewed from above; the Teifi coracle – illustrated here – has a pinched waist amidships, but the Tywi coracle is almost oval in shape. In the language of its users, the coracle is a cwrwgl; *the Irish have a boat made on similar lines – though much bigger – which they call* curach.

Llanddewi, Gower, West Glamorgan
Gower Farm Trails

P ⊕ A 4

One walk with three cut off points at different distances in West Gower that examines the working of farms and meets the farm's animals at close quarters.

Llanddewi, 12 miles W. of Swansea on a short minor road right from A4118, ¼ mile beyond Knelston village. Map sheet 159, reference 460890.

Jan.–Dec.   free.

Walk 1	2 miles	1 hour	4
Walk 2	5½ miles	3 hours	5
Walk 3	6 miles	3½ hours	5

Countryside Commission and West Glamorgan County Council.

Mr. V. Watters, Llanddewi Farm.

'Gower Farm Trail', 10p available at Swansea tourist information centres (see back) and locally.

Oxwich, Gower, West Glamorgan
Oxwich Sand Trail

P A 2

This trail in 8 stages traces the movement and influence of sand at Oxwich, where it comes from, where it goes and what happens when it meets water, plants, animals and people. It ends at Gower Countryside Centre.

Oxwich, 12 miles W. of Swansea on a minor road leaving A4118, 2 miles W. of Nicholaston. Map sheet 159, reference 502865.

Jan.–Dec.   1 mile   1 hour   free.

Nature Conservancy.

'Oxwich National Nature Reserve' free and 'Oxwich Sand Trail', free.

Port-Eynon, Gower, West Glamorgan
Port-Eynon Point Walk

P A 1

A walk through a National Trust Reserve with its sea-shore and limestone cliff, bird and plant life, and magnificent coast views.

Port-Eynon, village at W. extremity of A4118 road from Swansea, map sheet 159, reference 468850.

Jan.–Dec.   2¾ miles   2 hours   free.

National Trust and Glamorgan County Naturalists' Trust.

'Four Nature Walks in Glamorgan', from Glamorgan County Naturalists' Trust, c/o Nature Conservancy Council, 44 The Parade, Roath, Cardiff, Price 15p (plus 10p postage and packing) and from the following centre.

Rhosili, Gower, West Glamorgan
Gower Coast Nature Trail

P ⊕ A 1

Seven stations trace an interesting limestone flora, with glimpses of fulmars, petrels, guillemots and razor bills as well as the superb scenery of Rhosili Bay and Worms Head.

Rhosili, 15 miles W. of Swansea on B4247 – extension from Scurlage of A4118. Map sheet 159, reference 417881.

Jan.–Dec.   3 miles   3 hours free.

Nature Consevancy.

'A limestone nature trail, Gower Coast National Nature Reserve', Small charge.

Swansea, West Glamorgan
Discovering the Lower Swansea Valley

P ⇄ ⊕ A 7

Two heritage trails illustrating improvements in the environment in an area once noted for its extensive derelict land.

Pentrechwyth and Bonymaen E. side of the Tawe river, Swansea Map sheet 159, reference 678961.

Jan.–Dec.   free

Walk 1	2 miles	1½ hours
Walk 2	1½ miles	1½ hours

Swansea Heritage Committee.

'Discovering the Lower Swansea Valley', 10p, available at local information Centres (see back).

360

Swansea, West Glamorgan
Dylan Thomas' Uplands Trail

🅿 �#️ 💷 A 7

Dylan Thomas was born at
5 Cwmdonkin Drive on October
2nd 1914, in Swansea's Uplands,
a district of Swansea which still
abounds with places and buildings
referred to in his writings. This
trail takes you to many of them.

Uplands, 1 mile N.W. of
Swansea City Centre. Map sheet
159, reference 640933.

Jan.–Dec.   2 miles   2 hours   free.

Swansea Heritage Committee,
Swansea City Council and
Oakleigh House School.

'Dylan Thomas' Uplands
Trail', 10p, available locally.

361

Swansea, West Glamorgan
*Industrial Archaeology Trail,
Lower Swansea Valley*

◀ �#️ 💷 A 7

The trail, in 19 viewing points,
aims at placing the monuments
and sites in the context of the
area's history over the past two
and a half centuries. A 'sister'
pamphlet has been produced
which illustrates the reclamation
and conservation which is
currently converting the valley
into a place of beauty and
enjoyment.

From Royal Institution of
South Wales near Wind Street,
Swansea, to Landore along the
valley of the River Tawe. Map
sheet 159, reference 657928.

Jan.–Dec.   2¼ miles   3 hours   free.

Swansea Heritage Committee in
conjunction with Swansea City
Council Planning Dept.

'Industrial Archaeology Trail,
Lower Swansea Valley', 10p,
available locally.

362

Swansea, West Glamorgan
Morriston Trail

🅿 💷 A 7

A trail which illustrates the
history and townscape of a Welsh
working class chapel culture. The
trail is in two parts. The first
deals with Morris' Town proper
and an extension runs to Morris
Castle and Landore, an area rich
in industrial history.

Morriston, 3 miles N. of
Swansea City Centre on A4067.
Map sheet 159, reference 674979.

Jan.–Dec.   3 miles   2 hours   free.

Swansea Heritage Committee
in conjunction with Swansea City
Council and South Wales
Industrial Archaeology Society.

'Morris' Town Trail', 10p,
available locally.

363

Swansea, West Glamorgan
Swansea Town Trail

🅿 �#️ 💷 A 7

A trail of 18 interesting features
in the older part of Swansea, a
seaport and industrial city.

Swansea, West Glamorgan,
map sheet 159, reference 656930.

Jan.–Dec.   1½ miles   1 hour   free.

Swansea Heritage Committee in
conjunction with Swansea City
Council.

'Swansea Town Trail', 10p,
available locally.

364

Bishopston	575895	6
🅿 💷 B 1 5		

Bishopston, Pwlldu Bay, return
by Hunts Farm and Hael
(560876).

365

Carmarthen	409198	2
🅿 A 3 4		

From 409198 on the old
wharves at Carmarthen a path
follows the river W.S.W. and S.
to join B4312 at 402185. Return
same way or by road.

366

Carmarthen	417203	4
🅿 A 3 4		

From the Parade at Carmarthen,
417023 go E. and join path along
old leat to A40(T) at 428211.
Cross to path opposite, passing
hospital, to cross A485 and
continue to 427222. Return by
road passing Roman Amphitheatre.

367

Carmarthen	417023	2½
🅿 A 4		

From The Parade at Carmarthen,
417203 go E. to A40(T) at 423210.
Cross and go N. up Cwm Oernant
Road to reservoirs where a path
on L. goes N.W. and W. to a
road which follow to L. to
Springfield Road which follow to
town centre.

368

Carmarthen	421197	4½
🅿 A 4		

From 421197 N.E. (path
omitted from map) past Ty-gwyn
to road, N. to Llangunnor
Church. Take lane to 434200,
cross road to opposite lane
passing old lead mine engine
house and Nant. At 'T' junction
go W., at next 'T' junction S.E.
to A48(T) cross to F.P., S.W. to
427186, take lane W.N.W. and so
to Pensarn and lane to start.

369

Glanamman, nr. Ammanford	686135	5
🅿 A 6		

Glanamman (map sheet 159), up W.
side of Cwm Pedol on map sheet
160 to 695155, S., S.W. and N.W. to
Blaen Berach (back on map sheet
159) (679156) then S.W. to road,
then S. by road and path to
673142, E. to 682145 and back to
starting point.

370

Laugharne	302107	4
🅿 A 1 4		

Laugharne, E. and S. of and
then over St. John's Hill returning
by The Laques.

371

Laugharne	302107	4
P	A 2	

Laugharne, N.E. along the estuary returning by alternative paths and tracks.

372

Llandeilo	590196	4
P	A 4	

Golden Grove (4 miles S.W. of Llandeilo) W. below Allt Berach to Ty'r wern, 569193, S.W. to Glan Rhydw (573196) and B4300 and back up the road.

373

Llandybie	618155	7
P	B 6	

Llandybie, S.W. to Piodau-fawr, W.N.W. to 599160, N. to 598167. Then on road E.N.E. and continue on path to 610169, then S. via Pentre Gwenlais.

374

Llanelli	508033	3
P	A 3	

Llanelli (Hengoed) W. and S. down to Furnace Reservoir and back by alternative path to the road at Tydu Farm, 510025 and back.

375

Llanelli	518022	6–8
P	B 3 5	

Llanelli (Felinfoel) up W. side of Cwm Lliedi Reservoir, road to Cil-wnwg-Fawr (514051), path to Gelli-Galed and S. to Cil-wnwg-Fach (517047) and back.

376

Llanelli	546052	3
P	A 3 5	

From bridge 2¼ miles S. of Llannon go up W. side of Afon Morlais to A467 and back. This walk, through Forestry Commission land, starts from the picnic site but is not waymarked.

377

Llanmadoc	440933	5
P	A 2	

Llanmadoc, circuit of Whitford Burrows.

378

Llanstephan	353105	4
P	A 1 4	

From 353105 at Llanstephan (parking) go S. across beach for 100 yds., turn up lane to fence, path L. near coast to 346098. Go N.W. and then along track W.S.W. (not on 1:50,000 map) to Lord's Park, N.W. to 332105, then E. along road to 342106, path N. to road which cross to path E. and S.E. to village.

379

Oxwich	495866	4
P	A 1 5	

Oxwich, Oxwich Church, Oxwich Point, Oxwich Green and back.

380

Parkmill	545892	9
P	B 6	

Parkmill, N.W. to Cilibion, S.W. and S. to Cefn Bryn, Penmaen and back.

381

Pontardulais	580048	3
P	A 4	

Fforest near Pontardulais, N. past Fforest Hall and N.N.W. along ridge to Tyllwyd road and back on N.E. side of ridge to A483 at 582052.

382

Pontardulais	605045	8
P	A 6	

Pontardulais, Graig Fawr and Pen y Cwar, S. to Gelli-gwm Rock bearing W.S.W. then N. and W. to start.

383

Pontyberem	475129	5
P	A 4 6	

Crwbin (3 miles N.W. of Pontyberem) S.W. to Sychnant, 469124 Gelligatrog, to B4309 which follows N.W. to minor road through Velindre.

384

Pontyberem	480128	5
P	A 6	

Pontyberem over Mynydd Llangyndeyrn to Blaen Berem 498135 along road N. to hairpin, path to W. to Crwbin and back.

385

Rhosili	416881	4 or 3
P	⊕ A 1	

Rhosili to (1) N. to Hillend and back over the Down. (2) to Pitton via the coast, Talgarth's Well and back.

386

Rhosili	427877	4 or 8
P	⊕ A 1	

Pitton to Port-Eynon by the coast. Return by bus or by Little Hills, Paviland Manor and Pilton.

387

The Mumbles, Swansea	630875	
P	⊕ A 1	

Mumbles Head to Caswell Bay by the coast.

Map 160
Brecon Beacons

Brecon Beacons

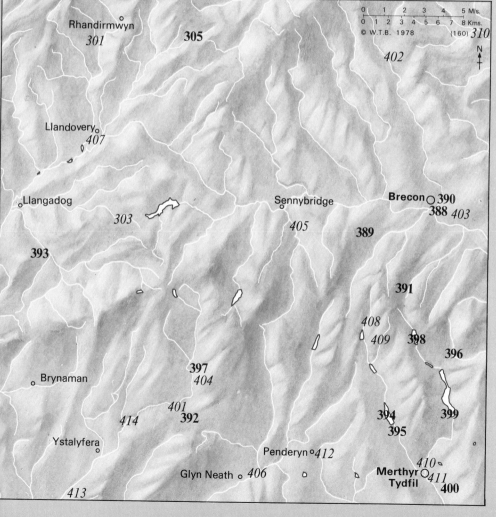

0   1   2   3   4   5 Mls.
0 1 2 3 4 5 6 7 8 Kms.
© W.T.B. 1978   (160) *310*

N

Rhandirmwyn
301   305   *402*

Llandovery
407

Llangadog   Sennybridge   Brecon ○ 390
                303   388 *403*
393   *405*   389

                                                        391

                                            408
                                            409 398
                                                        396
                        397
                        404
                                            394
        401   395
414   392
Ystalyfera   399
                        Penderyn ○ *412*
        Glyn Neath ○ *406*   *410*
                                        Merthyr ○ 411
                                        Tydfil   *400*
413

388

Brecon, Powys

A look at Brecon

P ⊖ A 7

A 28 point closer look at Brecon, ancient capital of Brecknock, which sits astride the Usk river in the Brecon Beacons National Park. The walk's high spots are the cathedral, castle remains, ancient narrow street pattern, museum and church.

Brecon, town centre, start from National Park Information Centre in Glamorgan Street. Map sheet 160, reference 045285.

Jan.–Dec. 1½ miles 1 hour free.

Brecon Beacons National Park Authority.

'A look at Brecon', 3p.

389

Brecon, Powys

Brecon Beacons National Park Mountain Centre, Libanus

P A 6

A small centre open daily consisting of an interpretive display, refreshment, toilet and rest areas, a little accommodation for organised groups and an information service, provided for the better understanding and enjoyment of the Park's facilities.

Mynydd Illtyd, a common 1 mile N.W. of Libanus, a village on A470 Brecon – Merthyr road 3½ miles S.W. of junction with A40. Map sheet 160, reference 977262.

Brecon Beacons National Park Authority.

Warden: On site. Tel. Brecon 3366.

390

Brecon, Powys

Some Short Walks around Brecon

P ⊖ A B 4 6

Eight walks from the Usk-side market town of Brecon to beauty spots, hilltops and places of interest in surrounding Brecon Beacons National Park.

Brecon, on A40. Map sheet 160, reference 045285.

Jan.–Dec. free.

River Usk Walk	1½ mls.	1 hr.
Priory Groves	2 miles	1½ hrs.
Canal Towpath	2½ mls.	1½ hrs.
Usk Promenade	2½ mls.	2 hrs.
Cantref	4 mls.	2¾ hrs.
Dinas ruins	5 mls.	3 hrs.
Pen y Erug Hill	5 mls.	3 hrs.
Ffrwdgrech Falls	6 mls.	4 hrs.

Brecon Beacons National Park Authority.

'Some short walks around Brecon', 3p.

391

Brecon, Powys

Walking in the Brecon Beacons

P ⊖ B C 6

Brecon Beacons National Park Committee have published an Information Sheet, No.25, price 3p, listing the chief walks to the peaks of the 2,950 feet high old red sandstone mountain range that dominates the National Park. Ten routes are listed:

Walks to Pen-y-Fan, the highest peak:

Map sheet 160:

From	Reference	Distance miles	Time hours
Bryn	080244	6¾	4½
Cefn Cyff	057240	5	3¾
'Gap' Road	036235	3½	2¾
Neuadd Res.	037170	3¼	2¼
Bryn Teg	036235	2½	2¼
Cwm Gwdi	024247	2¾	2½
Cwm Llwch	006244	3¼	2¾
Pen Milan	001249	3¾	3
Storey Arms	982203	2	1½
Y Gyrn	982203	3	2¼

A walk in Glyn Tarrell from:

Telephone box west of 'Storey Arms layby 2½ 1¼

Parking is very restricted at all starting points.

Brecon Beacons National Park Authority.

'Walking in the Beacons', 3p.

Note: Though open throughout the year the walker should beware of winter mists and snow.

392

Coelbren, Powys

Henrhyd Waterfall Walk

P A 3 5

(See also walk from reference 834126). A walk to the 90 feet high Henrhyd Waterfall on Nant Llech, a tributary of the upper Tawe on the S. edge of Brecon Beacons National Park.

Henrhyd Waterfall, Coelbren, 2 miles E. of Abercraf. Map sheet 160, reference 855119.

Jan.–Dec. ½ mile 1 hour free.

National Trust.

393

Llangadog, Dyfed

Penarthur Forest Walk

P A 5

Wooded slopes in the northern foothills of Carmarthen's Black Mountain, along the Sawdde tributary of the Towy, is the idyllic setting for this family-type walk.

Llangadog, on A4069. Start at Coed Ston Car Park, 2 miles south of Llangadog. Map sheet 160, reference 717255.

Jan.–Dec. ½ mile ¾ hour free

Forestry Commission.

Local Forester, Tel. Llanwrtyd Wells 202.

Waymarked.

394

Merthyr Tydfil, Mid Glamorgan

Garwnant Forest Walk

P ⊖ A 5

A walk through the conifer forest of Coed Taf in the Brecon Beacons National Park from Garwnant Forest Centre.

N.W. end of Llwyn-Onn Reservoir beside A470, 5½ miles N. of Merthyr Tydfil on Brecon road. Map sheet 160, reference 003131. Start from Garwnant Forest Centre.

Jan.–Dec. 2 miles 1 hour free

Forestry Commission.

Garwnant Forest Centre

The main objective of the Garwnant centre is to encourage visitors to venture out into the forest to enjoy themselves and to provide background information to help people understand the things they will see.

Models, photographs and a slide programme are used to set the forestry scene in relation to water supply, farming and the National Park. A circular forest walk starts from the centre.

In addition a lecture room has been provided for educational purposes where children will be able to study environmental subjects during wet weather and display their own work.

395

Merthyr Tydfil, Mid Glamorgan
Llwyn-Onn Reservoir Forest Walk

🅿 🚶 A 3 5

The Llwyn-Onn Walk explores the conifer forest of the Taf Valley, 1½ miles to the South of the Garwnant Forest Walk.

S.W. Corner of Llwyn-Onn Reservoir near dam, at a point just W. of A470, 4½ miles N. of Merthyr Tydfil on Brecon road. Map sheet 160, reference 009112.

Jan.–Dec. ½ mile ½ hour free.

Forestry Commission.

Thrift.

396

Merthyr Tydfil
Mid Glamorgan
Talybont Forest Walk

🅿 A B 5

Four separate trails exploring the afforested headwaters of the Caerfanell river, deep in the Brecon Beacons National Park.

Blaen-y-glyn, 8 miles N. of Merthyr Tydfil on the minor road to Talybont-on-Usk. Map sheet 160, reference 061171.

Jan.–Dec. free.
Waterfall
Walk (red) 1 ml. 1 hr.
Caerfanell
River Walk (blue) 2 ml. 1½ hr.
Barn Walk (green) 2 ml. 2hrs.
Fan Ddu Ridge
Walk (yellow) 3 ml. 2½ hrs
Forestry Commission.
'Talybont Forest Walks', hodfa Coedwig Talybont', 5p.

397

Penycae, Powys
Craig y Nos Country Park Walks

🅿 A 4 5

40 acres of woodland near Craig y Nos Castle – former home of the 19th century opera singer, Madam Adelina Patti – in the upper Swansea Valley, watered by the Tawe's headwaters, form the setting of the Park. ½ mile away are Dan yr Ogof show caves.

Craig y Nos, 6 miles north of Ystradgynlais on the A4067 Swansea – Sennybridge road. Map sheet 160, reference 840155.

Jan.–Dec. Various free.

Brecon Beacons National Park.

Supervisor on site. Tel. Abercrave 063977 395.

'Craig y Nos Country Park', a leaflet, free from Park Information Centres.

Special events in the park include demonstrations of country skills – e.g. sheep shearing and horseshoeing – a country fair and conducted walks.

398

Pontsticill, Merthyr Tydfil, Mid Glamorgan
Pont Cwm-y-Fedwen Forest Walk, Neuadd Reservoir

🅿 A 5

A forest walk high in the Taf Fechan Valley in the Brecon Beacons.

Neuadd Reservoir, 5 miles N. of Pontsticill, left off minor road near Ystrad Gynwyn. Map sheet 160, reference 031176.

Jan.–Dec. 2 miles 2 hours free.

Forestry Commission.

399

Pontsticill Mid Glamorgan
Taf Fechan Long Distance Walk

🅿 B 5 6

A waymarked walk of some 10 miles from a point near Taf Fechan Reservoir dam, N. by the W. bank to the Neuadd Reservoirs, then return along the E. bank of Taf Fechan Reservoir.

Pontsticill, 4 miles N. of Merthyr on minor road E. from A470 at Cefn-Coed-y-Cymmer. Map sheet 160, reference 056120.

Jan.–Dec. 10 miles 4 hours free.

Forestry Commission.

400

Taff Valley, Mid Glamorgan
Walks in the Taff Valley between Cardiff and Merthyr

🅿 🚲 🚶 A B C 5 6 7

A 50 mile Long Distance Walk in 20 points along the Valley of the Taff from the sea to its source, compiled by David Rees. Cardiff – Merthyr. Map sheets 160, 170 and 171.

Various public and private footpaths.

Jan.–Dec. 50 miles free.

'Walks in the Taff Valley', David Rees, price 90p, published by The Starling Press, Risca, Newport, Gwent.

401

| Abercraf | 834126 | 4 |

🅿 A 3 5

Abercraf (Llech Bridge), up E. and N. bank of Nant Llech to Henrhyd waterfall, N. to 847134, then W. and S.W. to Glyn-llech-isaf (842127) and back. (See also Henrhyd Waterfall Walk from 855119.)

402

| Brecon | 008406 | 13 |

🅿 C 6

Upper Chapel E. to Twyn-y-post (029409) Fforest (054412) Pantycolli (068407) Werntoe (073376) Ysgwydd Hŵch (053375), Twyn-y-post, and back. (This walk can be shortened at several places.)

403

| Brecon | 043286 | 7 |

🅿 🚶 B 3 4

Brecon town centre, bridge, follow path E. along S. bank of River Usk to Dinas, B4558 at 076266, return by canal path.

73

404

Craig-y-nos	845168	4

P A 6

Gwyn Arms, Pwll-coediog, S.S.W. then S.S.E. to Rhongyr-uchaf N.N.E. to Penwyllt, N.W. to Pwll-coediog.

405

Defynnog, nr. Sennybridge	922272	9

P C 6

From S.W. of Defynnog, over Fforest Fach, S. to Cray (895245), then N.E. to start.

406

Glyn-neath	901077	5

P B 3 5

Pont Nedd Fechan, road to 910079, path N., N.W. and N. to 916097, N.W. to Pont Melin-Fach, down W. bank of River Neath to start.

407

Llandovery	820390	6

P B 6

From 1 mile E. of Cynghordy E.N.E. across Afon Crychan, to Coed Cochin and 835393, then E. and N. to Scratch (847395). Drop to valley. W. to Afon Crychan at 838400 and back.

408

Merthyr	983203	10

P ⊕ C 6

Storey Arms, N. down old road to Old Glanrhyd (984240) continue to Modrydd, S. over Pen Milan (996230) Y Gyrn, and back.

409

Merthyr	005132	4–6

P ⊕ B 5 6

From N.E. corner of Llwyn Onn Reservoir (5 miles N.N.W. of Merthyr) take forestry road which eventually bears N. and climbs, return by Wernfawr (003138).

410

Merthyr Tydfil	030077	5

P ⊕ A 5 6

Cefn-coed-y-cymmer, N.N.W. to E. of Ffrwd-Uchaf on road to Forestry Gate, continue until track comes in from S.W. at about 009107. Take it (avoiding a right branch) to return to Ffwrd-Uchaf and back.

411

Merthyr Tydfil	055085	10

P ⊕ B 5 6

Merthyr (Galon Uchaf), Morlais Hill, Faenor Church, Nant Cwm-moel, Llwyn Onn Reservoir, bus back or cross dam, S. to Sychbant and Cefn-coed-y-cymmer, drop to Taf Fechan at 038076, follow up E. bank of river to road bridge at 045097 follow road S.E. to 049092 whence path to start.

Pollarded Willows

Great Reed Mace

Bur-Reed

Arrowhead

Bog Pond Weed

Wetlands — rivers, canals, lakes and reservoir banks.

Kingfisher

Willow

Heron

Moorhen

Coot

Water Soldier

Yellow Water-Lily

Frogbit

412

Penderyn	945085	5

🅿 B 3 5

Penderyn, Craig y Ddinas at 916082 N.W. and N. to Cilhepste-Cerig (925091) Hepste Waterfall 928100 and back.

413

Pontardawe	735055	7

🅿 B 6

Ynysmeudwy, Gellifowy, Gilwern Colliery (disused), (745089), Pant (733083) Cwm-nant-Lleiky and back.

414

Ystradgynlais	790110	8

🅿 B 5 6

Ystradgynlais, Cwmgiedd, 784130, Dorwen (772148) Tir-y-gof (772120) and back.

Map 161
Abergavenny and the
Black Mountains

Abergavenny and the Black Mountains

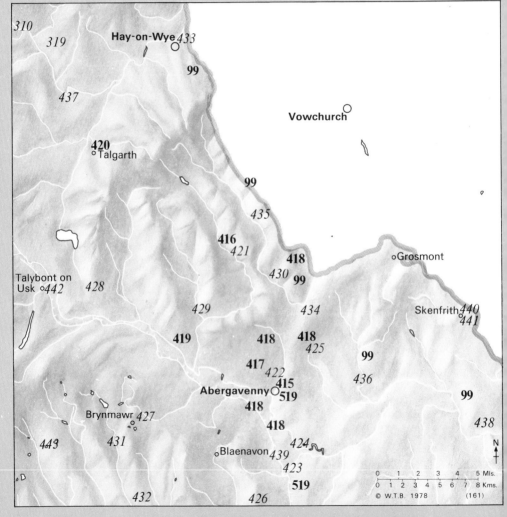

310

319

Hay-on-Wye *433*

99

437

Vowchurch

420
Talgarth

99

435

416
421

418

Grosmont

430 **99**

Talybont on
Usk *442*   *428*

429

434

Skenfrith *440*
441

419

418

418
425

99

417 *422*
415
Abergavenny **519**

436

99

518

Brynmawr *427*

518

438

443

431

Blaenavon *439*

424

99

423

519

N

432

426

0 1 2 3 4 5 Mls.
0 1 2 3 4 5 6 7 8 Kms.

© W.T.B. 1978   (161)

415

Abergavenny, Gwent
Civic Society Town Trail

🅿 🚻 ⬦ A 7

A tour of historic Abergavenny in twenty-two stages highlighting local history and architecture.

Abergavenny, on A40. Map sheet 161, reference 300142.

Jan.–Dec. 1 mile 1 hour free.

Abergavenny Civic Society.

'Abergavenny Town Trail', small charge, from Information Centre, Monk Street.

416

Abergavenny, Gwent
Mynydd Du Forest Walk

🅿 A 5

An 11-stage forest trail 150 acres through Ffawyddog Wood in the Black Mountains section of Brecon Beacons National Park. Ffawyddog comes from the Welsh for 'beech', and the area is rich in tree, plant and animal life.

Grwyne Fawr Valley, 2½ miles N.W. of Partrishow reached by a minor road N. from Abergavenny. Map sheet 161, reference 266252.

Jan.–Dec. 1½ miles 1½ hours free

Forestry Commission.

'Mynydd Du Forest Trail', 5p.

417

Abergavenny, Gwent
St. Mary's Vale Nature Trail

🅿 B 6

A 7-stage trail exploring a steep-sided tree-covered valley and open moorland on Sugar Loaf hill in the Black Mountains region of Brecon Beacons National Park.

St. Mary's Vale, reached by minor road through Llwyn Du, 1½ miles N.W. of Abergavenny, a town on A40. Map sheet 161, reference 284162. Start ½ mile W. of Llwyn Du reservoir reached by Chapel Road and Pentre Road from the Brecon road out of Abergavenny.

Jan.–Dec. 2 miles 1½ hours free.

Brecon Beacons National Park Authority and National Trust.

'St. Mary's Vale Nature Trail', 2p.

418

Abergavenny, Gwent
30 Walks in the Abergavenny area

🅿 🚻 ⬦ A B C 6

The Abergavenny area of the Brecon Beacons National Park has much of landscape value within its relatively small area of 51 sq. miles. Mixed farmland, high rolling hills, attractive villages, historic buildings, and the only canal within a National Park, combine in a district of charming variety. The lively and interesting market town of Abergavenny lies on the fringe of the Park and forms an excellent centre from which to reach on foot, or by bus or car, the starting points of the selected walks. Some of the routes are waymarked with orange arrows, which are to assist walkers particularly across enclosed farmland. White waymarks, if seen, indicate other rights of way which are not part of the '30 walks'. Offa's Dyke Long Distance Footpath is marked by oak sign-posts and white acorn waymarks. Many rights of way in the area are at present indicated by green sign-posts at the roadsides. Some of these coincide with the walks described here.

Signposts mark the route of the Offa's Dyke footpath from Chepstow to Prestatyn.

Abergavenny Gwent Map sheets 161, 171.

Walk	Length Miles	Time hours
1. *Llanover Slopes*	4	2
2. *Canal Towpath*	5–8	2–3
3. *Llanellen Slopes*	3	1–1½
4. *Blaenavon Mountain*	6	3
5. *Llanellen-Llanfoist*	7	3½–4
6. *Blorenge Mountain (Route 1)*	5	3–4
7. *Blorenge Mountain (Route 2)*	6	3–4
8. *Fiddler's Elbow and River Usk*	3	1½–2
9. *River Usk and Llanwenarth*	4½	2–3
10. *Sugar Loaf by Mynydd Llanwenarth*	7	3½
11. *Sugar Loaf by Rholben Spur*	6	3
12. *Sugar Loaf by Rholben*	6	3
13. *Sugar Loaf by Llwyn Du*	6	3
14. *Sugar Loaf by The Deri*	9	4
15. *Sugar Loaf by Park Lodge*	7–9	3–4
16. *Sugar Loaf from Fforest*	5	2–2½
17. *Dial Garreg from Fforest*	6	3
18. *Partrishow, Cwmyoy from Fforest*	8	4–4½
19. *Oldcastle from Llanfihangel Crucorney*	6	3–4
20. *Skirrid Fawr*	3	2
21. *Llanthony Priory Slopes*	2	1
22. *Llanthony Valley Slopes (Route 1)*	4	2
23. *Llanthony Valley Slopes (Route 2)*	4½	2–2½
24. *Northern part Llanthony Valley*	7	3–3½
25. *Bal Mawr from Llanthony*	4½	2–3½
26. *Garn Wen Ridge*	6–7	3½–4
27. *Cwm Llanwenarth*	4	2
28. *Llangenny to Sugar Loaf*	5	3
29. *Offa's Dyke footpath around Pandy*	4	2
30. *Mynydd Du Forest*	11	6

Brecon Beacons National Park Authority with Ramblers Association. 'Thirty walks in the Abergavenny area', 8p.

Bridge over the Usk near Crickhowell. This is one of the Brecon Beacons' finest walking areas.

419

Crickhowell, Powys
A look at Crickhowell

P ⊕ A 7

21 interesting features – houses, church, castle – mark this walk through Crickhowell from the Square to Porthmawr, the site of the ancient 'Great Gate'.

Crickhowell, 6 miles west of Abergavenny on A40(T). Map sheet 161, reference 218184.

Jan.–Dec. 1½ miles 1 hour free.

Crickhowell Community Council and Brecon Beacons National Park Authority.

'A look at Crickhowell', 3p.

420

Talgarth, Powys
A look at Talgarth

P ⊕ A 7

A leisurely walk around 30 points in the interesting old market town of Talgarth on the River Enig in the lee of the Black Mountains.

Talgarth on A479, 8 miles east of Brecon. Map sheet 161, reference 155337.

Jan.–Dec. 1 mile 1 hour free.

Brecon Beacons National Park Authority.

'A look at Talgarth', 3p.

421

Abergavenny 252287 5

P B 5 6

From a point 5 miles N.W. of Partrishow along valley to Grwyne Fawr Reservoir; return by alternative route.

422

Abergavenny 292160 6

P B 6

From Llwyn-du, 1 mile N.N.W. of Abergavenny, go up lane and left of Llwyn-du Farm, Park Lodge, and up by stream to track to the Deri. Various paths back.

423

Abergavenny 309082 3

P A 3

Rhyd-y-meirch (4 miles S. of Abergavenny on A4042), Tow Path, Dan-yr-heol, road to 297076, Ty-to-maen (300076) path to Rhyd-y-meirch.

424

Abergavenny 319094 4

P A 4

Llanover Church, cross Usk, Llangattock, Pant-y-Goytre Bridge and back starting on S. bank of Usk.

425

Abergavenny 330164 3–6

P B 6

From a point 2¼ miles N.E. of Abergavenny on B4521, climb to the path circling Ysgyryd Fawr and ascend to the summit, also do the circle.

426

Abersychan 270042 5

P ⊕ B 6

Abersychan (Nant y Mailor) E. and N.E., Goose and Cuckoo (290073 on Map sheet 161), Coed cae Du (300063), continue to 294052, then W. to start.

427

Brynmawr 202125 8

P B 5 6

Brynmawr along the 'shelf' road, or by Disgwylfa to Pant-y-rhiw (205157) and Daren Cilau, return by 204144.

428

Bwlch 140226 12

P C 6

Bwlch, N.W. by Roman Road, Allt yr Esgair, Llangorse Village, Long Cairn, at 161285 S. by either side of Mynydd Llangorse to Cefn Moel (159241) and back.

429

| Crickhowell | 240205 | 7 |

P **B** 5 6

Llanbedr (2½ miles N.E. of Crickhowell) N.E. over Blaen-yr-henbant to just beyond Disgwylfa (263235). Return to Blaenau (243234) and Milaid or by Partrishow.

430

| Cwmyoy, nr. Abergavenny | 298233 | 9 |

P **C** 6

Cwmyoy, Daren (farm), Weild, Maesyberan, E.N.E. to 308269, Offa's Dyke Path along Hatterrall Ridge and Hill, and back.

431

| Ebbw Vale | 175086 | 3 |

P ⊕ **A** 6

Ebbw Vale, Morning Star Inn, (178091) S. to 180075, N.E. to Mynydd Carn-y-cefn and back.

432

| Ebbw Vale | 185055 | 4 |

P ⊕ **B** 6

Cwm (2 miles S. of Ebbw Vale), Ty'n-y-gelli (187072), S. to Cefn yr Arail to 198044, back by hillside path.

433

| Hay on Wye | — | 4½ |

P **A** 4 6

Clock Tower, Brecon Road S.W. to 226419 and follow Offa's Dyke S. for 1½ miles past Penyrwrladd chambered tomb to lane (226398). Follow this back to Hay on Wye (O.D.A.).

434

| Llanfihangel Crucorney | 285211 | 6 |

P **B** 6

Pont-yspig (2½ miles W. of Llanfihangel Crucorney), Dial-garreg (284241) Penrhiw (304222) and back.

Llanthony Priory's graceful arches blend beautifully with the landscape of the Black Mountains in the Breacon Beacons National Park.

435

| Llanthony | 288277 | 4 |

P **B** 6

Priory (288277) ½ mile N.E. to path slanting uphill in S.E. direction to reach Offa's Dyke at 308270. N. along path for 1 mile to 298285, then W. and S. to start. (O.D.A.).

436

| Llantilio Crossenny, Talycoed | 416152 | Various |

P **A** 5

Forestry Commission car park and picnic site. No waymarked walk but interesting walk by forest roads.

437

| Llyswen | 133378 | 7 |

P **B** 3 5

Llyswen, Brechfa Pool (119377) N. to Cefn Gafros Common (105410), back by various routes.

438

| Monmouth | 485107 | 6 |

P **B** 4

Wonastow, turn N.E. along road for ¼ mile then follow path left to King's Wood and tower at 479135. Return by alternative paths.

439

| Pontypool | 315057 | 5 |

P ⊞ ⊕ **A** 3 4

Bridge Farm (Goytre near Pontypool), N. along canal, cross at 309074 to go up Gwenffrwd stream, to road at 298077, S.W. to Goose and Cuckoo, S.E. to Coedcae Du (300063) back via 309057.

440

| Skenfrith | 456202 | 4 |

P **A** 4

Skenfrith to 465203, Hilston Tower, Crossway, Tre-gout and back.

441

| Skenfrith | 456202 | 4 |

P **A** 4

Skenfrith to 455210, Coed-y-pwll, Norton and back.

442

| Talybont-on-Usk | 115225 | 10 |

P **C** 3 5 6

Talybont-on-Usk, track to S. under Craig Dan-y-wenallt, follow until it reaches road in about 4 miles at 101175. Turn back to Bwlch-y-waun (115189), drop at Cwm Crawnon and return along canal.

443

| Tredegar | 145088 | 6 |

P ⊕ **B** 6

Tredegar, Mount Pleasant, Pont gwaith-yr-haearn, Cefn Manmoel to 165054, return by Fountain Inn.

Map 162
Gloucester and
Forest of Dean

Monmouth and Tintern

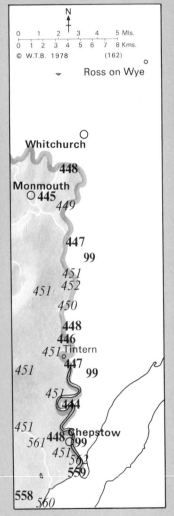

N

0 1 2 3 4 5 Mls.

0 1 2 3 4 5 6 7 8 Kms.

(162)

Ross on Wye

Whitchurch

448

Monmouth

○ **445**

449

447

99

451

451 *452*

450

448

446

451 Tintern

447 **99**

451

451

448

451

444

451

Chepstow

561 **448** ○**99**

451

502

559

558 *560*

444

Chepstow Gwent
Wyndcliff Nature Trail, St. Arvans

P A 5 6

A trail through Blackcliff and Wyndcliff Forest Nature Reserve to a 700 feet high viewpoint over the Wye to the sea.

Wyndcliff on A466, ½ mile beyond St. Arvans, a village 1½ miles N. of Chepstow. Map sheet 162, reference 523971.

Jan.–Dec. ¾ mile 1 hour free.

Gwent Trust for Nature Conservation, Nature Conservancy and Forestry Commission.

'Wyndcliff Nature Trail', 2p.

445

Offa's Dyke Path
Castles alternative

B 4 5 6

From Monmouth (Sheet 162) to a point near Hay on Wye (Sheet 161) walkers on Offa's Dyke Path (see Sheet 116 section for main information) have an alternative that takes in castles both sides of the Wales/England border. Prepared by the Offa's Dyke Association, maps of the route together with detailed instructions are available, price 15p, from:

Offa's Dyke Association, Old Primary School, West Street, Knighton, Powys.

446

Tintern, Gwent
Barbadoes Hill Forest Walk

P ⊕ B 5

A demanding walk with vantage points over the lower Wye Valley.

Tintern, on A466, 6 miles N. of Chepstow. Map sheet 162, reference 524004.

Jan.–Dec. 2 miles 2 hours free.

Forestry Commission.

'A walk in Tintern Forest', 5p.

447

Tintern, Gwent
Chapel Hill Forest Walk

P ⊕ A 5

A forest walk of 7 stages in the beautiful Wye Valley from Tintern. Can be combined with visit to Tintern Abbey.

Tintern, on A466, 6 miles N. of Chepstow. Map sheet 162, reference 524004.

Jan.–Dec. 1½ miles 1½ hours free.

Forestry Commission.

'A Walk in Tintern Forest', 5p.

448

Wye Valley, Gwent
Wye Valley Walk, Chepstow to Symonds Yat

P 🚉 ⊕ A B 5

The walk provides a variety of views and interests from high up above the valley floor to village centres, wooded areas and riverside banks in this part of the Wye Valley designated an Area of Outstanding Natural Beauty.

Kingsmark School, Chepstow. Map sheet 162, reference 531942, to Symonds Yat Station, Map sheet 162, reference 561159.

Jan.–Dec. 21½ miles Can be free. taken in stages

Gwent County Council with Gloucester, Hereford and Worcester County Councils.

'Wye Valley Walk', 5p plus postage.

This walk is currently being extended north to Ross-on-Wye.

449

Monmouth	510130	6

P	⊛	B	3	6

Monmouth W. to Kymin Hill Follow Offa's Dyke path to B4231 road, 2 miles S.E. then right to Redbrook and riverside path back to Monmouth (O.D.A.).

450

Tintern	525042	3

P	A	5

Llandogo, Cuckoo Wood, 533055, Moon Cottage (528053) Cleddon, drop to Llandogo. Note: In part previously a Forest Trail, but descriptive pamphlets out of print.

451

Tintern Forest
Walks and picnic facilities

P	A	5

The Forestry Commission's pamphlet 'Recreation facilities in

Horehound

Tintern Forest', 5p, gives full information on these sites.

Chepstow, St. Pierre Great Wood	505930	Various

Picnic place and small car park. Easy waymarked forest walk of 1 hour.

Chepstow, Great Barnet's Wood	513943	Various

Picnic place and car park. Various rambles on two forest roads and in beech/larch woodlands.

Walk from Mounton (reference 513932) takes in this area.

Chepstow, Cockshoots	517945	Various

Walks from a small parking area. Beech woodland and lime burning pits, partially restored by Forestry Commission. Walk from reference 513932 takes in this area.

Chepstow, Fryth Wood	515953	1 mile

¾ hour walk from small car park in a 79 acre woodland.

Shirenewton, Pryscau Bach	495943	Various

Car park and picnic area with toilets at start of three waymarked forest walks.

St. Arvans, Fedw Wood	508985	Various

Picnic site, children's play area and toilets at start of waymarked forest walk to Fairoak pond, of about 1½ hours.

Devauden, Chepstow Park Wood	501985	Various

Parking place, used by horse-boxes of riders using Chepstow Park Wood Riding Route. Rambles in woodland. Walk from Shirenewton (reference 485961) takes in this area.

St. Arvans, Lower Wyndcliff	527972	Various

Views of Horseshoe Bend on River Wye from sylvan picnic site on A466. Start of 365 steps walk to Upper Wyndcliff. (See also Wyndcliff Nature Trail, from reference 523971.)

Tintern, Angiddy 526002 Valley Walk		

From Forestry Commission's Sawmills car park, serving Barbadoes Wood Walk and Chapel Hill Walk, take start of Chapel Hill Walk and follow the orange and black marker pegs up Angiddy Valley to Pant-y-Saeson (1½ hours there and back) linking sites of a once thriving industrial complex based on water power.

Tintern, Whitestone	524028	Various

Car parking and toilets at start of waymarked walks leading to views of the Wye and the best areas to see the largest variety of trees.

Trelleck, Beacon Hill	511054	Various

Car park and picnic site at start of short waymarked walk to Beacon Hill (1,000 feet high)

Trelleck, Maryland	521055	Various

Parking area at start of way-marked forest walk of about 2 hours.

Whitebrook, Manor Wood	529059	Various

Car park in ancient Beech Wood at start of waymarked walk to restored Manor Wood pond, a relic of a 17th century industrial complex.

452

Whitebrook	535065	5

P	A	3	5

Whitebrook, along Wye to 535091, up road almost to Lone Farm (526091) path S. to Tregagle and back.

Map 170
The Rhondda

The Rhondda

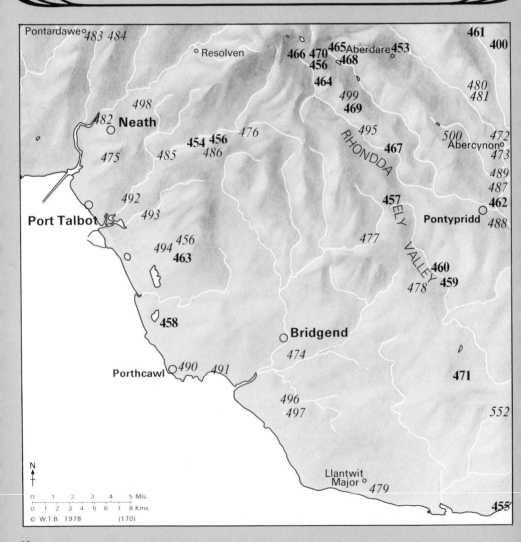

453

Aberdare, Mid Glamorgan
Walks in Dare Valley Country Park

P **⊕** **A** **5** **6**

A Countryside Park created in 1972 in a valley now being returned to its original wooded and green state. 2 walks and 4 waymarked trails explore an area rich in natural history and industrial archaeology. One of the trails is suitable for disabled persons in wheelchairs.

On W. of Aberdare, reached by A4059, 23 miles N. of Cardiff. Access by car is from A4059 N. of Trecynon, through Cwmdare, or from B4277 at Highland Place (off Monk St.). Map sheet 170, reference 982028.

Jan.–Dec.   1–5 miles   free.

Cynon Valley District Council and Countryside Commission. Warden on site. Tel. Aberdare 4672.

'Dare Valley Country Park', free on site.

454

Afan Valley, Port Talbot, West Glamorgan
Afan Argoed Country Park Walks

P **⊕** **5** **6**

Six waymarked walks, of varying distances, examine the forest trees, plants and terrain in the most beautiful part of the Afan Valley's scenic route. To record the facts and recapture the spirit of eventful times in the history of Coal Mining a purpose-built museum has been constructed at the country park. It has interesting displays, a simulated coal face and pit gear from an era now ended in the Afan Valley.

6 miles N.E. of Port Talbot on Afan Valley road, Port Talbot – Cymmer, A4107. Map sheet 170, reference 821951. Start at Countryside Centre.

Jan.–Dec.   free.

Old Parish Walk	1 ml.	45 mins.
Larch Walk	1½ mls.	60 mins.
Nant Cynon Walk	1 ml.	45 mins.
Gyfylchi Tunnel Walk	1½ mls.	1½ hrs.
Riverside Walk	2 mls.	2 hrs.
Argoed Trail	2½ mls.	3 hrs.
Michaelston Trail	5 miles	3½ hrs.

The 23-miles long **Coed Morgannwg Way**, running from Rhigos Mountain, near Hirwaun, to Margam Park at Port Talbot passes through the Afan Argoed Country Park.

Wayfarer Course at Afan Argoed

The Forestry Commission, in conjunction with Swansea Bay Orienteering Club have laid out a Wayfaring Orienteering Course in the forest at Afan Argoed.

A number of marker posts (controls) are set out in the forest and participants use a map to find their way from one to another, and so around the course.

Information and Wayfarers pack for Margam Forest (small charge) are available from the Afan Argoed Countryside Centre.

West Glamorgan County Council and Forestry Commission.

'Afan Argoed Park, Forest Walks'. 10p. Further walks are in course of preparation.

455

Barry, South Glamorgan
Porthkerry Country Park

P **A** **1** **2** **5**

The Park comprises 250 acres mainly of wooded slopes with a large grass area in the valley which runs down to the sea, Porthkerry Bay, at the S.W. end. The valley is extensively used for informal family recreation. Porthkerry Wood was designated a site of Special Scientific Interest by the Nature Conservancy in October, 1962. The Cliff (Bull Cliff) includes fossil strata and is partially clothed with dense wind-moulded scrub. Some cliff nesting birds breed on the cliffs below the Bulwarks.

Porthkerry, 2 miles W. of Barry. Map sheet 170, reference 086668. Park Road entrance walking or car. Mill Wood entrance off Nant Talwg Way, walking only.

Jan.–Dec.   2 miles   1 hour   free.

Vale of Glamorgan Borough Council.

Warden: Mr. Cedric Lloyd, Nightingale Cottage, Porthkerry Country Park. Tel. Barry 3589.

456

Coed Morgannwg,
Mid Glamorgan
Coed Morgannwg Way (Forest Walk) Rhigos, nr. Hirwaun, to Margam Park

P **B** **C** **5** **6**

A 23 miles, long distance walk, opened in June 1977 by the Forestry Commission, the Coed Morgannwg Way traverses the hills and valleys of a particularly attractive part of South Wales which overlays the coalfield. At about the halfway point it passes through Afan Argoed Country Park where there is a museum of the Mining Industry.

Craig-y-llyn, Rhigos Mountain, 3 miles N.W. of Treherbert. Map sheet 170, reference 924031 to Margam Park, 3 miles E. of Port Talbot, map sheet 170, reference 813849.

Jan.–Dec. 23 miles 12 hours free.

Forestry Commission, West Glamorgan County Council and Mrs. G. M. Brown.

Guide book in course of preparation.

457

Gilfach Goch, Mid Glamorgan
Industrial Trail

P **A** **7**

The setting for Richard Llywelyn's 'How Green was my Valley', Gilfach Goch was reborn with the landscaping recently of its scarred hillsides. Interesting colliery remains have been retained forming the basis of a fascinating tour of a typical valleys' town.

Gilfach Goch, 6 miles N.W. of Llantrisant on B4564. Map sheet 170, reference 983895.

Jan.–Dec. 2 miles 1½ hours free.

Mid Glamorgan County Council.

'Gilfach Goch Industrial Trail', available.

Walkers interested in exploring the industrial heritage of the Rhondda Valley, just over the hill from Gilfach Goch, should obtain the Wales Tourist Board's booklet on Industrial Archaeology (see address at back of book).

Duneland, estuary banks and foreshore.

Golden-Eye Ducks

Oyster Catchers

Sea Rocket

Razor Shell

458

Kenfig, near Porthcawl, Mid Glamorgan
Kenfig Burrows Walk

🅿 A 2

Three miles of sand dune footpath to the sea and back, with strange seashore plants, flowers of the dunelands and birds of the coast. This is one of several walks in the recently designated Kenfig Burrows Nature Reserve.

Kenfig Burrows, reached by minor road through Maudlam village S.W. from Pyle, 5½ miles W. of Bridgend on A48. Map sheet 170, reference 803812.

Jan.–Dec. 1½ miles 3 hours free.

The Glamorgan County Naturalists' Trust.

Warden on site.

'Four Nature Walks in Glamorgan', from Glamorgan County Naturalists' Trust, c/o Nature Conservancy Council, 44 The Parade, Roath, Cardiff. Price 15p (plus 10p postage and packing).

Temporarily out of print.

459

Llantrisant, Mid Glamorgan
Mynydd Garth Maelwg Walks

🅿 A 5 6

A series of unwaymarked forest paths between Talbot Green and Coed Ely overlooking the Vale of Glamorgan.

Car park and picnic area at Map sheet 170, reference 024846.
Forestry Commission.

460

Llantrisant Mid Glamorgan
Trecastell Walks

🅿 A 5 6

Wayfaring course and a series of forest walks from Tyle Garw, Pontyclun. Main entrance, Map sheet 170, reference 029817.

Forestry Commission.

Maps can be obtained from Honesty Box in garden of Forester's house, Symlog, Pontyclun, ½ mile east of start of course, at Map sheet 170, reference 030842.

Teal

Shelduck

Ringed Plover

Sea Holly

Sea Rocket

Sandpiper

Whelk

Starfish

Bladder-Wrack

85

461

Merthyr Tydfil, Mid
Glamorgan
Old Glamorgan Canal Walk, Abercanaid

P A 4 5

The booklet covering the 4-mile circuit tells the story of a now-abandoned canal and mines which are being absorbed into the wooded landscape of the Taff Valley.

Abercanaid, 1 mile S. of Merthyr Tydfil, off A470. Map sheet 170, reference 047062.

Jan.–Dec. 4 miles 3 hours free.

Glamorgan Naturalists' Trust.

'Nature Walks in Glamorgan – 3 walks in the coalfield', from Glamorgan Naturalists' Trust, c/o Nature Conservancy Council, 44 The Parade, Roath, Cardiff. Price 15p (plus 10p postage and packing).

462

Pontypridd, Mid Glamorgan
Walk on Mynydd Eglwysilan

P A 6

Three miles of hillside footpath above Pontypridd, giving panoramic views of the Taff and Rhondda Valleys.

Hospital Road, ½ mile E. of Pontypridd, 10 miles N. of Cardiff on A470 dual carriageway. Map sheet 170, reference 083091.

Jan.–Dec. 3 miles 2½ hours free.

Glamorgan County Naturalists' Trust.

'Nature Walks in Glamorgan – 3 walks in the coalfield', from Glamorgan Naturalists' Trust, c/o Nature Conservancy Council, 44 The Parade, Roath, Cardiff. Price 10p (plus 10p postage and packing).

463

Port Talbot, West
Glamorgan
Walks in Margam Park, Margam

P A 5

An 823 acre estate varying from bracken, pastureland and wood-land to ornate 18th century Orangery Gardens forming a recently opened Country Park. Herd of fallow deer.

Margam, 1 mile E. of Margam Works entrance at Port Talbot on A48. Map sheet 170, reference 8086.

Jan.–Dec. various various free.

West Glamorgan County Council.

Warden on site.

'Margam Park', 30p.

Other brochures also available.

464

Rhondda, Mid Glamorgan
Blaen Rhondda Walk

P B 6

A 2-mile waymarked cross country route exploring natural and man-made features of the rugged upper reaches of the Rhondda Valley.

3 miles N.W. of Treherbert on A4061 Treorchy to Hirwaun road, Map sheet 170, reference 922021.

Jan.–Dec. 2–3 miles 3 hours free.

Glamorgan County Naturalists' Trust and Forestry Commission.

'Nature Walks in Glamorgan – 3 walks in the coalfield', from Glamorgan Naturalists' Trust, c/o Nature Conservancy Council, 44 The Parade, Roath, Cardiff. Price 15p (plus 10p postage and packing).

465

Rhondda, Mid Glamorgan
Cefn Glas Short Walk

P A 5 6

One of the many attractive moorland and forest walks on the col between Treherbert in the Rhondda and Hirwaun in the Dare Valley.

Mynydd Beili-glas, Rhondda on A4061. Map sheet 170, reference 922025.

Jan.–Dec. 1 mile 1 hour free.

Forestry Commission and Mid Glamorgan County Council.

'Cefn Glas Short Walk', free from Visitor Centre at start of walk in August only.

466

Rhondda, Mid Glamorgan
Graig Llyn Ridge Walk

P A 5 6

The col separating the Rhondda Valley from the Aberdare and Neath Valleys is a high wild and wooded world.

Waymarked in red, the Graig Llyn walk follows a ridge giving panoramic views. Mynydd Beili-glas, Rhondda, on Treherbert to Hirwaun road A4061. Map sheet 170, reference 922025.

Jan.–Dec. 2½ miles 1½ hours free.

Forestry Commission and Mid Glamorgan County Council.

'Graig Llyn Ridge Walk', free leaflet available from Visitor Centre at start of walk in August only.

467

Rhondda, Mid Glamorgan
Graig Nantgwidden Walks, Gelli

P ⬡ ⊕ A 5

The wooded W. slopes of the Rhondda Valley at Llwynypia form the setting for this waymarked forest walk.

Llwynypia on B4223 junction with A4119 Cardiff – Rhondda road, 1 mile N. of Tonypandy. Map sheet 170, reference 988945.

Jan.–Dec. 1½ miles 1 hour free

Forestry Commission.

Not waymarked. Map in car park.

468

Rhondda, Mid Glamorgan
Lluest Walk/Cefn Bryn Gelli Long Walk

P B 5 6

Starting from the same spot as the Graig Llyn Ridge Walk, this walk waymarked in orange, heads east to Lluestwen reservoir, the headwaters of the Rhondda Fach.

Mynydd Beili-glas, Rhondda, on Treherbert to Hirwaun road A4061. Map sheet 170, reference 922025.

Jan.–Dec. 4 miles 2½ hours free

Forestry Commission and Mid Glamorgan County Council.

'Lluestwen/Cefn Bryn Gelli', free leaflet from Visitor Centre at start of walk in August only.

469

Rhondda, Mid Glamorgan
Rediscover Rhondda: 3 walks

P   B   5   6

Three walks on the hills surrounding Treorchy, Rhondda's famous musical town, have been mapped out for us by members of the town's Youth Centre.
Start: Stag Hotel, Treorchy. Map sheet 170, reference 959965.
Open   Jan.–Dec.

1	Bwlch-y-Clawdd Walk	5–6 mls.	3+ Free
2	Cwm Saerbren Walk	5–6 mls.	3+ Free
3	Lluest Wen Reservoir Walk	7–8 mls.	4 Free

Treorchy Youth Centre in conjunction with Forestry Commission, various societies and Local Councils.

'Rediscover Rhondda', 15p available locally.

470

Rhondda, Mid Glamorgan
Rhondda Visitor Centre

P   A   5   6

Open each August, the Forestry Commission, in conjunction with Local Councils, the Rhondda Society, Glamorgan Naturalists' Trust and National Museum of Wales, organise a series of guided walks from the Centre. Panoramas, waterfalls, geology and general scenery are viewed, with experts explaining finer points.

To the west of A4061 between Treherbert to Hirwaun road in the vicinity of map sheet 170, reference 922025.

Minibus service connects the centre with Treherbert Station during open dates in August.

Watch for announcements on the Rhondda Forest Project under which 16-seater safari landrovers convey visitors to Craig-y-llyn, Pen-pych, Lluest-wen Reservoir and Fforch-orky.

Information on the Centre and programme is available from the Forestry Commission, or from the Mid Glamorgan County Council by telephone: Cardiff 28033 (Ext. 433) or Porth 2476 (Ext. 218).

471

Welsh St. Donat's near
Cowbridge, South Glamorgan
Tair Onen Forest Walks

P   A   5

Two walks through the forests of South Glamorgan's lowland Vale.

Welsh St. Donat's 3 miles N.E. of Cowbridge reached by minor road E. off A4222, ½ mile N. of Aberthin village. Map sheet 170, reference 031768. Picnic areas at Map references 031768 and 036763.
Jan.–Dec 1–2 miles ½–1 hour free.

Forestry Commission.

Forest Office, Bonvilston.
Tel. 241.

'A walk in Tair Onen Forest', 5p.

472

Abercynon	077945	3
P A 6		

Abercynon, Daren y Foel, S.W. to Pen y Foel (070945), return N. and E. by alternative paths by Gilfach-y-rhyd.

473

Abercynon	083956	5
P A 3 6		

Abercynon, W. to Cefn-glas and Pont-y-Gwaith (080976) old railway track to Quaker's Yard up to canal and back, or follow the Taff.

474

Bridgend	904795	6
P ⬚ ⊕ B 3 5		

Bridgend to Merthyr Mawr, along the river to sheep wash bridge, cross, path left in 300 yards, Merthyr Mawr footbridge over Ogmore river, Ewenny River, Verville and back.

475

Briton Ferry	750954	
P ⊕ A 5		

Briton Ferry (Ynys-y-maerdy) S.S.W. along forest road to Queen's Walk and surrounding woods.

476

Cymmer	862963	3
P ⊕ A 5 6		

From Cymmer almost circular walk partly on roads round Mynydd Rhiw-llech in Cymmer Forest.

477

Llandyfodwg, Bridgend	956872	5
P B 5 6		

Llandyfodwg, up Cwm Dimbath to 962905, back by Mynydd-y-Gwair or Mynydd Maendy.

478

Llanharan	002832	4 or 6
P B 6		

Llanharan Church, E.N.E. to The Beacons, Mynydd Meiros and back or drop towards 025845 and take forestry road to N. of Mynydd Meiros and back on paths S.

479

Llantwit Major	955674	3
P A 1 2		

Llantwit Major (Col-huw Bay), W. along the rocks or cliffs to St. Donats and back.

480

Mountain Ash	035020	4
P ⊕ B 6		

Ffynnon-y-gog over Cefn Pennar (044025) to Merthyr Tydfil or Abercanaid.

481

Mountain Ash 052988 3

📱 A 6

Mountain Ash (Navigation) to Twyn Brynbychan (064989) return by alternative path to Newtown.

482

Neath 740987 4

📱 A 6 7

By way of Neath Abbey or Bryn Coch over Mynydd Drumau (725995) to Glais via 723009.

483

Pontardawe 745045 7

📱 B 5 6

Cilybebyll, Crynant Forest, over ridge towards Varteg Hill, drop E. to Blaenant-Meurig (778066) S. and W. by Forestry Roads.

484

Pontardawe 745045 5

📱 A 4 6

Cilybebyll Church, Gellinudd, The Mill, Rhos, Alltwen along ridge to Graig Gellinudd and back.

485

Pont-rhyd-y-fen 798942 2–6

📱 B 5

Pont-rhyd-y-fen into Michaelston Forest N. of Afon Afan or from Afan Argoed car park 821951, dropping to and crossing river.

486

Pont-rhyd-y-fen 821951 5

📱 ⊕ B 5 6

Afan Argoed car park, track up to Pen Disgwylfa (826934) Penhydd Fawr (807931) and back.

487

Pontypridd 058909 5

📱 ⊟ ⊕ B 5 6

Hopkinstown (1 mile N.W. of Pontypridd) N. to Glog, Tai'r Heol 065928, and back via 063908.

488

Pontypridd 085895 5

📱 A 6

Glyntaff, S.E. to church at 106890, N.W. to 095908 W. and S. via The Common (080903) and back.

489

Pontypridd 086926 3

📱 A 6

Cilfynydd up Nant Cae-dudwg to Cwm-bach (108933) return by Carneddi Llwydion, W. T. Tower (097911) then to 092908 and back N.W. direction or follow road.

490

Porthcawl 815765 7

📱 ⊕ B 1 2

Porthcawl, Sker Point (788798) Kenfig Pool and Church, E. to South Cornelly and bus.

491

Porthcawl 835775 5

📱 ⊕ B 1 2

Newton, E. over Cwm y Gaer, Candleston Castle (872773) and back through Merthyr Mawr warren.

492

Port Talbot 765905 3

📱 ⊟ ⊕ A 6

Port Talbot, follow the forestry road round Mynydd Dinas.

493

Port Talbot 790872 6

📱 ⊕ B 6

Brombil Valley, Tumulus (798888) to 793893, turn W. for 1 mile and return S.E. by path above and parallel to M4.

494

Port Talbot 799863 6–8

📱 B 5 6

Margam Abbey; N.E. over Mynydd–Margam (819890) to Maesteg (851903) or Bryn (819920) or return by way of Cwm Philip (818875).

495

Rhondda 970955 7

📱 ⊟ ⊕ B 6

Ton-Pentre, W.S.W. 3 miles to Craig Ogwr at 925953, E.N.E. to Cwm-parc and back.

496

St. Bride's Major, nr. Bridgend 893750 3

📱 A 4 7

St. Bride's Major to Ogmore Castle (883769) and back.

497

St. Bride's Major, nr. Bridgend 897752 4

📱 A 4

St. Bride's Major N. to Old Castle Down, S.E. to Castle-upon-Alun, and back due W. by alternative path.

498

Tonna, nr. Neath 775990 8

📱 B 5 6

Tonna S. around Ivy Tower (776983) across Pelenna Forest to 818998 dropping to Melincourt Brook and waterfall, return by Ystradowen and towpath.

499

Treherbert 923030 5

📱 B 5 6

Mynydd Beili-glas, W. to Craig y Pant tumulus (896036) drop N. to 900043 and follow Forestry Commission road to start.

500

Ynysybwl 030955

📱 A 5

Llanwonno Church, N.W. to 019976, S.E. to Pistyll-goleu at 033963 and back.

Map 171
Cardiff and Newport

Cardiff and Newport

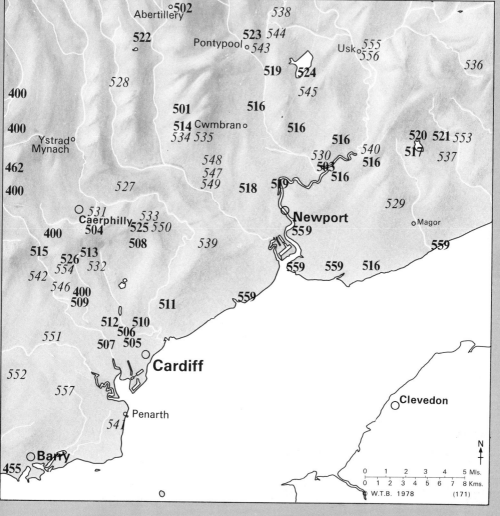

502
Abertillery 538
522 523 544
Pontypool 543
519 524
Usk 555
556
536
528
400
501 516
400 514 Cwmbran
534 535
516
516 520 521 553
517 537
Ystrad Mynach
548
547
549
530 540
503 516
516
462
400 527 518 519 529
531 533
Caerphilly 525 550
504 508 539
Newport
559
Magor
400
515 513
526 532
542 554
546 400
509
511
559 559 516
559
512 510
506
507 505
559
Cardiff
551
552
557
Penarth
541
Clevedon
Barry
455

N

0 1 2 3 4 5 Mls.
0 1 2 3 4 5 6 7 8 Kms.
W.T.B. 1978 (171)

501

Abercarn, Gwent
Cwm Gwyddon Forest Walk

🅿 ⊕ A 5

A 4-stage walk on steep, forested upper reaches of Nant Gwyddon, a tributary of the River Ebbw, to view its forest, bird and plant life.

Abercarn, 7 miles N.W. of junction 27 off M4 motorway at Newport, Gwent, on A467 Newport – Brynmawr road. Map sheet 171, reference 238959.

Jan.–Dec. 2 miles 1½ hours free.

Forestry Commission.

502

Abertillery, Gwent
Town Trail

🅿 ⊕ A 7

The ribbon-shaped town of Abertillery winds its way uphill between the heights of Mynydd yr Arael and Cefn bach. Red brick houses hug the contours; In the valley bottom are colliery workings. This walk gives the close up of the main features of a typical valley environment.

Abertillery, on A467 Newport (Gwent) to Brynmawr road. Map sheet 171, reference 2104.

Jan.–Dec. 7 miles 3 hours free.

Gwent County Council and Abertillery and District Museum Society.

'Abertillery Town Trail', brochure, small charge.

Waymarked.

503

Caerleon, Gwent
Caerleon Heritage Trail

🅿 ⊕ A 7

A walk through a town which was once the Roman Legionary fortress, Isca.

Caerleon, on B4236, 3 miles N. of Newport, Gwent. Map sheet 171, reference 340906.

Jan.–Dec. 1 mile 2 hours free.

Caerleon's Civic Society, Local History Society and Gwent County Council.

'Caerleon, fortress of the Legion', 35p, available at Amphitheatre; 'Caerleon Heritage Trail', 10p plus postage from Gwent County Council, County Hall, Cwmbran.

(Small entrance charge to Roman remains).

504

Caerphilly, Mid Glamorgan
Caerphilly Common Nature Trail

🅿 ⊕ A 6

A 7-stage trail along a limestone ridge on the S. edge of the coalfield.

Heathland, with heather and bilberries, limestone plants and exposed rock formations, as well as wide views of South Wales, are found here.

Caerphilly Common, on A469 Cardiff to Caerphilly road, 5 miles N. of Cardiff, Map sheet 171, reference 156853.

Jan.–Dec. 1 mile 1 hour free.

Cardiff and Rhymney Valley District Council Glamorgan County Naturalists' Trust.

'Caerphilly Common', 15p.

505

Cardiff, South Glamorgan
A walk in Central Cardiff

🅿 ⊜ ⊕ A 7

A thorough brochure giving a 50 point walk taking in the remains of Roman and Mediaeval Cardiff, the renowned Civic Centre group of buildings and the newly-paved pedestrian areas of the Shopping Centre.

Cardiff City Centre, starting at the Post Office in Westgate Street near Central Station. Map sheet 171, reference 183761.

County of South Glamorgan and Principality Building Society.

Jan.–Dec. 1½ miles 2 hours free.*

'A walk in Cardiff', small charge. From the Council and Tourist Information Centre in Cardiff.

*There is a charge for entering Cardiff Castle and many of the buildings listed can only be viewed from the outside.

506

Cardiff, South Glamorgan
Bute Park Nature Trail

🅿 ⊜ ⊕ A 5

Twenty-one stages in a way-marked walk through Bute Park's 350 acres of formal and informal gardens and grounds alongside the River Taff from Cardiff Castle to Blackweir.

Bute Park, Castle Street alongside Cardiff Castle. Map sheet 171, reference 178765.

Jan.–Dec. 2 miles 1½ hours free.

Cardiff City Council (Parks Department).

'Bute Park Nature Trail', 15p.

507

Cardiff, South Glamorgan
Canton to Llandaff Walk

🅿 ⊜ ⊕ A 5 7

The walk is divided into 4 sections, which may be taken one at a time or as a continuous walk through Victoria Park, Thompsons Park, Llandaff Fields and Llandaff Court.

Cowbridge Road, W. of City Centre, Map sheet 171, reference 155769.

Jan.–Dec. 3 miles 2½–3 hours free

Cardiff City Council (Parks Department)

'Canton to Llandaff Walk' from Cardiff City Parks Department.

508

Cardiff, South Glamorgan
Cefn-Onn Walk, Llanishen

🅿 ⊜ ⊕ A 5

In early summer this walk, through glades of almost every type of rhododendron and azalea, is an unforgettable experience.

Parc Cefn-Onn, a Country Park on the N.E. edge of Cardiff. 1 mile E. along minor road off A469, Cardiff – Caerphilly road 3 miles N. of Gabalfa interchange with A470. Map sheet 171, reference 178838.

Jan.–Dec. 1¼ miles 1½ hours free

Cardiff City Council (Parks Department).

'Cefn-Onn Walk', 5p.

509

Cardiff, South Glamorgan
Glamorgan Canal Wharf

P ⊕ A 3

A booklet which introduces the walker to the rich bird and water-plant life along the banks of the disused Glamorgan Canal, now scheduled as a Nature Reserve.

W. of Whitchurch Hospital, Velindre Road, reached off A4054 in Whitchurch, 2 miles N. of Cardiff. Map sheet 171, reference 144805.

Jan.–Dec. ¾ mile 2 hours free.

Glamorgan County Naturalists' Trust and Cardiff City Council (Parks Department).

'Four walks in Glamorgan', from Glamorgan County Naturalists' Trust, c/o Nature Conservancy Council, 44 The Parade, Roath, Cardiff. Price 15p (plus 10p postage and packing). 'Glamorgan Canal Nature Reserve', 10p from Cardiff City Parks Department.

510

Cardiff, South Glamorgan
Nant Fawr Walk

P ≋ ⊕ A 3

The walker traces the path of the Nant Fawr brook in Cardiff – through Waterloo Gardens, Roath Recreation Ground, Roath Park Botanic and Pleasure Gardens and alongside Roath Lake.

N.W. Cardiff, 1 mile from City Centre. Map sheet 171, reference 197779.

Jan.–Dec. 3 miles 2–3 hours free.

Cardiff City Council (Parks Department).

'Nant Fawr Walk', 5p.

511

Cardiff, South Glamorgan
Rhymney Walk

P ⊕ A 4

A walk in Cardiff's eastern outskirts through Rhymney Hill Gardens.

Newport Road, Rumney, E. outskirts of the city. Map sheet 171, reference 2179.

Jan.–Dec. 3 miles 2½–3 hours free.

Cardiff City Council (Parks Department).

'The Rhymney Walk', small charge.

512

Cardiff, South Glamorgan
Taff Valley Walk

P ≋ ⊕ A 4 7

A long walk through the Castle Grounds divided into sections, and taking in part of the Glamorgan Canal Nature Reserve.

Cardiff City Centre through the Castle Grounds – North Gate. Map sheet 171, reference 181768.

Jan.–Dec. 5 miles 3–4 hours free.

Cardiff City Council (Parks Department).

'The Taff Valley Walk', small charge.

513

Cardiff, South Glamorgan
Wenallt Nature Trails

P ⊕ A 5

Two trails of 12 and 14 stages on a woodland ridge with view over the plain around Cardiff. Open woodland and heath plants grow in profusion.

Wenallt Hill reached 1 mile down a minor road S.S.W. from Travellers Rest Inn, 5½ miles N. of Cardiff on A469 Cardiff – Caerphilly Road. Map sheet 171, reference 153833.

Jan.–Dec. 1 mile 1 hour free.

Cardiff City (Parks Department), Rhymney Valley District Council and Glamorgan Naturalists' Trust.

'Wenallt Nature Trail', 15p.

514

Cwmcarn, Gwent
Cwmcarn Scenic Forest Drive and Walks

P ⊕ A B 5 6

Though designed as a 7 miles car drive, there are many opportunities for exhilarating walks up to 1,370 feet on the forested mountains overlooking the River Ebbw and Newport, in Gwent. There are wide views, ancient

cairns, bird, plant and forest life, as well as picnic areas and adventure play areas for children.

Cwmcarn on A467. Newport – Brynmawr road 6 miles N.W. of interchange No. 27 with M4 motorway at Newport, Gwent. Map sheet 171, reference 238934.

Easter to Oct.   Various Charge.

Forestry Commission and Countryside Commission.

Forest Office, Craig Wen, Abercarn. Tel. Abercarn 223.

'Cwmcarn Scenic Forest Drive', from Information Booth on site.

515

Gwaelod-y-Garth, Mid Glamorgan
Great Garth Walk

P ≋ ⊕ B 6

A steep footpath climbs to heather-covered moorland with extensive views over the lower vale of the Taff.

Gwaelod-y-garth, on a minor road W. off A470 at interchange just N. of Tongwynlais, 5 miles N. of Cardiff. Map sheet 171, reference 110834.

Jan.–Dec. 2 miles 2½ hours free.

Glamorgan County Naturalists' Trust.

'4 Nature Walks in Glamorgan', from Glamorgan County Naturalists' Trust, c/o Nature Conservancy Council, 44 The Parade, Roath, Cardiff, price 15p (plus 10p postage and packing).

516

Gwent Walks

P B 4

A series of walks in the hills, woodlands and coastal reens of the County of Gwent. Several leaflets are planned. The first two now available, cover walks from:

Leaflet No. 1

Walk 1: Upper Cwmbran Walk. Map sheet 172, reference 274969.
2½ miles   1½ hours

Walk 2: Little Porton Walk.
Map sheet 172,
reference 375822.
4 miles   2½ hours
Walk 3: Llanbeder Walk.
Map sheet 171,
reference 388908
3½ miles   2 hours

Leaflet No. 2

Walk 4: Llanhennock – Glen
Usk – Ivybridge Walk.
Map sheet 171,
reference 353927.
2½ miles   1½ hours
Walk 5: Llanfrechfa –
Roughton Walk.
Map sheet 171,
reference 317937.
3 miles   2 hours
Walk 6: St. Julian's Park –
Cock O'North.
Map sheet 171,
reference 335888.
3½ miles   2 hours

Gwent County Council in
association with Ramblers'
Association (South Gwent Group).

'Walks in Gwent', 5p plus
postage.

517

Newport, Gwent
*Gray Hill Countryside Trail,
Wentwood Reservoir*

P A 5 6

A varied walk of forest, hill-
commons, a quarry and plantations with their associated bird
and plant life.

Wentwood Reservoir on minor
road 2 miles N. of Penhow, a
village on A48, 4 miles E. of
Coldra; exit No. 24 off motorway
M4 at Newport. Map sheet 171,
reference 428939.

Jan.–Dec. 2 miles 1½–2 hours free.

Gwent County Council.

'Gray Hill Countryside Trail',
2p.

518

Newport, Gwent
*14 Locks Picnic Site and
Interpretation Centre*

P A 7

The picnic site and interpretation
centre has been developed to
preserve the canal at Fourteen
Locks. This, the most impressive

engineering feat on the former
Monmouthshire Canal's Crumlin
branch.

Newport, leave M4 by exit 27
for A467 towards Risca. After
½ mile turn right for Henllys.
Picnic area is ¼ mile along this
road. Map sheet 171, reference
279886.

An interpretative trail is being
established here.

Gwent County Council.

Brochure available at
Interpretation Centre.

519

Newport, Gwent
*Usk Valley Walk: Newport to
Abergavenny*

A B 3 4

A walk along the eastern fringe
of the mountain block of South
Wales. It has been waymarked
throughout from Caerleon to
Abergavenny.

Newport Castle (Gwent) Map
sheet 171, reference 313884 to
Abergavenny Castle 1.2.3. Map
sheet 161, reference 299141.

Jan–Dec. 23 miles Can be free.
taken in parts

Gwent County Council.

Waymarked.

520

Newport, Gwent
Walks in Wentwood Forest

P A 5

Five waymarked walks in a
3,000 acre forest whose royal
hunting associations go back to the
Native Welsh Princes of Gwent.

Wentwood Forest, 8 miles N.E.
of Newport, reached by minor
road N. from Penhow on A48,
4 miles E. of M4 Coldra exit
No. 24. Map sheet 171.

Walk	Length	Time
1	1¼ miles	40 mins.
2	1½ miles	45 mins.
3	1 mile	30 mins.
4	2 miles	1 hour
5	4 miles	2 hours

Gwent County Council and
Forestry Commission.

'Walking in Wentwood Forest',
5p.

521

Newport, Gwent
Wayfaring in Wentwood

P A 5

Wayfaring is an ideal way to
explore the forest. There are up to
20 or 30 different controls on
each wayfarer course, which is
laid out over an area of about
1 sq. mile of the forest. Usually
the course has been designed to
take in scenic attractions of the
forest. By using your map you
can select a route to suit your
performance. If you cover only a
few controls on your first visit you
can plan alternative routes on
future visits.

Wentwood Course is at
Wentwood Lodge car park, map
171, reference 418945.

Jan.–Dec. 1½ mls. Varies   free
with skill

Contact: Forestry Commission,
Wentwood Forest, near Penhow,
Gwent. Tel. Penhow 265.

Wayfaring pack of map, control
sheet and plastic cover, 30p, on
site.

522

Oakdale, Gwent
*Pen-y-fan Pond Country Park
Walks*

P A 3 6

The Country Park lies in
pleasant countryside 1,000 feet
above sea level (325 metres)
on the plateau between the
valleys of the Sirhowy and Ebbw
Fawr. Pen-y-fan Pond was built
in the early 1800's as a 'feeder-
pond' to provide a regular water
supply to compensate for water
lost through locks from the
Crumlin area of the Monmouthshire Canal. The feeder channel
from Pen-y-fan Pond to Crumlin
can still be traced for much of the
way. Besides boating, sailing and
canoeing there are good public
paths and a 2 mile walk north-
wards up the ridge to Manmoel.

The main road to the pond is
from the south via the new
industrial estate road, off the
B4251 Blackwood to Crumlin
Road. Map sheet 171, reference
195005.

Jan.–Dec.   Various Walks   free
Gwent County Council and

Islwyn Borough Council.

'Pen-y-fan Pond Country Park', free, from Gwent County Council.

523

Pontypool, Gwent
A walk in Pontypool Park

 P ⬛ ⊡ A 4 7

A walk in eleven stages from Pontypool's leisure centre around one of South Wales' finest parks. The walk traces its origins and development from an 18th century private estate to a modern leisure area.

Pontypool, on A4051, Newport to Abergavenny road. Map sheet 171, reference 285005.

Jan.–Dec. 1½ mls. or 1½ hrs. free.
2¼ mls.
according
to route
chosen.

Gwent County Council and Borough of Torfaen Museums Service.

'A Walk in Pontypool Park', free from kiosk at Leisure Centre.

524

Pontypool, Gwent
Llandegfedd Reservoir Walks

P A 3 4

Five walks, totalling 18 miles in varied scenery of hills and woods, steep valleys and small villages.

Llandegfedd Reservoir, 3 miles E. of Pontypool reached by minor road from New Inn, Pontypool or W. from Usk through Llanbadoc. Map sheet 171. Start Eastern picnic area reference 329985, or Sor Brook picnic area, reference 323978.

Walk	Length	Time	Suitable
1	2¾ mls.	1½–2 hours	4
2	3¼ mls.	1½–2 hours	4
3	2½ mls.	1½–1¾ hours	4
4	3¾ mls.	1¾–2 hours	4
5	5½ mls.	2–2½ hours	5

Gwent County Council.

'Llandegfedd – Suggested Walks', 5p.

Llandegfedd reservoir, location for a series of walks organised by the Gwent County Council. (see item 524).

525

Rudry, nr. Caerphilly, Mid Glamorgan
Woodland Walks near Draethen

P A 5

Four walks through Coed Coesau Whips providing panoramic views over the Bristol Channel.

Rudry, 2½ miles E. of Caerphilly. Map sheet 171.

Walk coloured:

	Green	White	Red	Orange
Start from	Llwyncelyn Car Park, S. of Rudry at 201853			West of Maenllwyd Inn at 200865
Length	1 mile	2 miles	2 miles	1¼ miles
Walking time	1 hour	2 hours	2 hours	1½ hours
Open	Jan.–Dec.	Jan.–Dec.	Jan.–Dec.	Jan.–Dec.
Charge for entry	Free	Free	Free	Free

Forestry Commission, local forester. Tel. Newbridge 244223 or Caerphilly 882367.

'Woodland Walks near Draethaen', 10p.

526

Tongwynlais, Near Cardiff
South Glamorgan
Castell Coch Walks

P A 5

Unwaymarked walks in hilly wooded country from a car park and picnic site near Castell Coch, the castle in the trees at Tongwynlais, 5 miles north of Cardiff.

Side road N.E. from Tongwynlais for 1½ miles. Map sheet 171, reference 143839.

Jan.–Dec. Various walks free.

Forestry Commission.

527

Bedwas	171893	7

P ⊡ B 6

Bedwas, W. on path S. of railway to road which follows N. to 160905, back over Mynydd Dimlaith, N. to 162918, S.E. to Mynydd-y-Grug and back.

528

Blackwood	180032	4

P ⊕ A 6

Manmoel (4½ miles N. of Blackwood) S. down Nant y Felyn down Sirhowy then up side-stream to Pen-y-fan Farm (190015), or to Pen-y-fan Pond. Return over Mynydd Pen-y-fan.

529

Bishton, nr. Newport	392877	4

P A 4

Bishton, W. to Milton, Llanwern Church (371878) and back, or via Underwood and Waltwood Hill.

530

Caerleon	329913	6

P ⊕ B 4

Caerleon, N.W. to Park Farm, Llantarnam Church, A4042 N. over bridge, path to Llanfrechfa, 325937, Ponthir, cross Afon Lwyd, path to 325914 or instead of going to Llanfrechfa, follow Afon Lwyd to Ponthir.

531

Caerphilly	166867	5

P ≋ ⊕ A 6

N.E. and E. 1½ miles to Garth Place, S. over Mynydd Rudry, S.W. through Wern Ddu and The Warren, then N. to start.

532

Cardiff	153833	6

P ⊕ B 5 6

Wenallt car park, or the Deri, to Castell Coch and back.

533

Cardiff	178837	5

P ≋ ⊕ A 5

Cefn-Onn station or car park up track W. side of railway to Rudry Church and back.

534

Cwmcarn	215935	4

P ⊕ A 6

Cwmcarn over to Mynyddislwyn Church, N.E. on road, then tracks to Penrhiw-darren (208950) and back.

535

Cwmcarn	240935	To taste

P ⊕ A 6

Cwmcarn: (1) Up Nant Carn and back by different tracks. (2) S. to Pegwn-y-Bwlch follow track round Medart. (3) Drop to 235921 from Pegwn-y-Bwlch and take track W. via Cwm-byr (231921) winding around the base of Medart to start.

536

Devauden, Kilgwrrwg Common	469978	Various

P A 4 5

Car park, picnic area, children's play area and good views of Black Mountains of Gwent.

537

Llanfair Discoed, nr. Newport	427940	4

P A 5

Forester's Oaks, Gray Hill, N. to Bicca Common 445948, cross stream to follow track and road to 442958 S.W. to The Five Paths, and back. (See also Grays Hill Nature Trail.)

538

Mamhilad, nr. Pontypool	305034	5

P A 3

Mamhilad, Tow Path, to 305042 then path to 302053, up stream to Holywell, Garn Wen, back by Mamhilad Road.

539

Michaelston-y-Fedw, nr. Newport	230845	4

P A 4

Cefn Mably Park to 216833 S.

and N.E. to 225832 St. Julian's Farm and back along Rhymney

540

Newport	375908	4

P A 4

Cat's Ash near Newport, Kemeys Folly, drop at 394935 to forestry road and return along Kemeys Graig. (Route partly same as Llanbedr Walk from 388908 organised by Gwent County Council.)

541

Penarth	187704	6

P ≋ ⊕ A 1

Penarth, Lavernock Point, turn inland at church (187682) for ¼ mile for footpath by chalet park to Swanbridge and Sully (170674).

542

Pentyrch	100822	4

P ⊕ A 6

Pentyrch W. to Pen-llwyn, N.W. to Ty'n-y-coed N. and E. to Soar and back.

543

Pontypool	274025	4

P ≋ ⊕ A 5

Pontypool Hospital, N. through Lasgarn Wood to 282045. Path S. to track at 282039, follow to 279033, then drop S.W. towards hospital. (See also map sheet 171, reference 270042.)

544

Pontypool	291006	5

P ≋ ⊕ A 4

Pontypool Park, The Folly (295025) drop N.E. to canal at Mamhilad and return along it.

545

Pontypool	318970	5

P A 3 4

From a point ¾ mile E. of Pontnewydd and 1 mile S. of Llandegfedd Reservoir, N. to

Sluvad and back or go E. on road to 324990 where there is a path to 324977, cross stream to path S. to 327968 and back.

546

Radyr	132805	6

P ⚡ ⊕ B 4 6

Radyr, Pantawel (117809), Pentyrch, N. and E. of Garth Wood to Morganstown for return.

547

Risca	237905	5

P ⊕ A 6

Risca along W. bank of river, Black Vein and Ty'n-y-ffynnon, 206909 and back over Mynydd Machen.

548

Risca	240910	5

P ⊕ B 6

Risca (Penrhiw) path or track to Twmbarlwm road, then 253925 S.E. to Cwrt Henllys, past Reservoir, Craig y Merchant, 258904 and down to and along canal bank.

549

Risca	245895	3

P ⊕ A 6

S. for a circuit of Coed Mawr, return on path on W. side or by track from 238890.

550

Rudry, nr. Caerphilly	202853	3

P A 5

Forestry car park 1 mile S. of Rudry to Rudry Church, Maenllwyd Inn (201866) and back.

551

St. Fagans	120770	4

P ⊕ A 4

St. Fagan's, W. to St. George's Church, S. and E. to Michaelston-uper-Ely Church and back.

552

St. Nicholas, Cardiff	092743	2
	(on map sheet 171)	

P A 4

St. Nicholas, N.W. to Kingsland (082753) W. and S. to 080746, back by minor road and or paths.

553

Shirenewton, nr. Chepstow	485961	4

P A 4 5

Start 2 miles N. of Shirenewton N.E. to Pen-y-Parc (on map sheet 162) and back through Chepstow Park Wood.

554

Tongwynlais	131826	6

P ⊕ B 5 6

Castell Coch, Bwlch-y-cwm, Black Cock, 144848, Craig-yr-Allt (134851) Glan-y-llyn and back.

555

Usk	346028	5

P ⊕ A 5

Monkswood, N. and N.E., River Usk follow to Chain Bridge, S.W. and S. to Llan and Twyn Cecil, back through Cefn Mawr at 335033.

556

Usk	377010	5

P ⊕ A 4

Usk, Beech Hill, N. for 2 miles to Gwehelog and back.

557

Wenvoe	123730	6

P ⊕ B 4

Wenvoe, Michaelston-le-Pit, Dinas Powis. Back by alternative path and roads passing near Golf Course, Beauville and Wrinstone.

Castell Coch is a mediaeval site recreated as a castle in the late 19th century. Fine walks near it are covered by item No. 526.

Map 172
Bristol and Bath

Chepstow and Caldicot

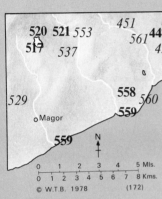

520 521 553   451   448 Chepstow
517   537   561   499
             451 562
                559
529   558
             560
     o Magor   559
       559
        N

0 1 2 3 4 5 Mls.
0 1 2 3 4 5 6 7 8 Kms.
© W.T.B. 1978   (172)

558

Caldicot, Gwent
Caldicot Castle Country Park

P ⊕ **A 4**

A 50 acre Country Park in the grounds of the Castle provides a beautiful setting for leisurely walks. Besides a car park, there are picnic sites and toilet facilities.

Caldicot, 5 miles S.W. of Chepstow on B4245. Map sheet 172, reference 487885.

Jan.–Dec.   Various walks   free.

Monmouth District Council and Gwent County Council.

Warden on site.

559

Chepstow, Gwent
Chepstow to Newport Coastal Walk

P **B 1 2**

A walk has been established along the Severn Estuary from Chepstow to Newport. Waymarked at present from Goldcliff (map sheet 171, reference 373820) to Black Rock (map sheet 171, reference 512880).

Jan.–Dec. 15 miles Can be free. taken in parts

Gwent County Council.

An extension of the route to Chepstow is being considered.

560

Chepstow	513882	5

P **A 2 4**

Black Rock, St. Pierre Pill, back same way, or N. of railway, or to Mathern, St. Pierre, to road at 510898.

561

Chepstow	513932	6

P **B 4 5**

Mounton, N.N.W. to Howick, E. along road to Fryth Wood, S. to start via Great Barnets Woods.

562

Chepstow	536936	8

P ⇌ ⊕ **B 4 7**

Chepstow, The Bulwarks, along Wye and under railway to Thornwell, under M4, walk to centre of Severn Bridge, Innage (525912) and back, or back direct.

Chepstow Castle, starting point for Offa's Dyke footpath and gateway to the Wye Valley area of outstanding natural beauty.

Birdwatching at Water Supply Reservoirs

Information by kind permission of the Water Space Amenity Commission.

WELSH WATER AUTHORITY

CARMARTHENSHIRE WATER DIVISION
Stradey Park, Llanelli, Dyfed

	Map	Ref	General location
Lliedi	159	512046	*N. Llanelli*
Llyn-y-Fan Fach	160	803218	*S.E. Llandovery*

CONWAY VALLEY WATER DIVISION
Glan Conway Corner, Colwyn Bay, Clwyd

	Map	Ref	General location
Llyn Elsi	115	783554	*S. Betws-y-Coed*

DEE & CLWYD RIVER DIVISION
Shire Hall, Mold

	Map	Ref	General location
Alwen	116	940540	*S.W. Denbigh*
Brenig	116	980560	*S.W. Denbigh*
Llyn Celyn	124	860405	*nr. Bala*

WEST DENBIGHSHIRE & WEST FLINT UNIT
P.O. Box 2, Plastirion, Russell Road, Rhyl, Clwyd

	Map	Ref	General location
Aled Isaf	116	910590	*S.W. Denbigh*
Dolwen	116	973704	*N.W. Denbigh*
Llyn Aled	116	920570	*S.W. Denbigh*
Llyn Conwy	115	780460	*N.E. Blaenau Ffestiniog*
Plas Uchaf	116	969710	*N.W. Denbigh*

GLAMORGAN WATER DIVISION
86 The Kingsway, Swansea

	Map	Ref	General location
Brianne	147	805500	*W. Builth Wells*
Cefn Cwrt	170	754940	*E. Swansea*
Cray	160	884216	*S.E. Llandovery*
Gnoll B	170	764972	*E. Swansea*
Lliw (upper)	159	662063	*N. Swansea*
Usk	160	825289	*S.E. Llandovery*
Ystradfellte	160	948180	*N.W. Merthyr Tydfil*

GWENT WATER DIVISION
Station Buildings, Station Approach, Newport, Gwent

	Map	Ref	General location
Talybont	161	100190	*N. Merthyr Tydfil*
Wentwood	171	431930	*E. Newport*
Ynysyfro (upper)	171	282891	*nr. Newport*

MERIONETH WATER DIVISION
Glyn Malden, Dolgellau, Gwynedd

	Map	Ref	General location
Llyn Bodlyn	124	648240	*N.W. Dolgellau*

Apply first to the Water Division for a permit needed to visit this reservoir.

	Map	Ref	General location
Llyn Cynwych	124	738208	*N. Dolgellau*
Llyn Eiddew Mawr	124	645337	*S. Blaenau Ffestiniog*
Llyn Gelli Gain	124	735328	*S. Blaenau Ffestiniog*
Llyn Tecwyn Uchaf	124	640381	*S.W. Blaenau Ffestiniog*
Llyn-y-Fedw	124	625330	*S. Blaenau Ffestiniog*

SOUTH EAST BRECONSHIRE WATER DIVISION
St. John's Mount, Pendre, Brecon

	Map	Ref	General location
Cairn Mound	161	201136	*W. Abergavenny*

TAFF WATER DIVISION
Pentwyn Road, Nelson, Treharris, Glamorgan

	Map	Ref	General location
Beacons	160	987185	*N.W. Merthyr Tydfil*
Cantref	160	994157	*nr. Merthyr Tydfil*
Castell Nos	170	963004	*nr. Rhondda*
Lisvane	171	189821	*nr. Cardiff*
Llandegfedd	171	330997	*E. Pontypool*
Llanishen	171	187817	*nr. Cardiff*
Lluest Wen	170	948018	*nr. Rhondda*
Llyn Fawr	170	918035	*nr. Rhondda*
Llwyn-on	160	007120	*N.W. Merthyr Tydfil*
Penderyn	160	938072	*W. Merthyr Tydfil*
Pentwyn	160	052150	*N. Merthyr Tydfil*
Pontsticill	160	056140	*N. Merthyr Tydfil*
Rhymney Bridge	161	103104	*N.E. Merthyr Tydfil*

WEST GWYNEDD WATER DIVISION
Bron Castell, High Street, Bangor, Gwyned

	Map	Ref	General location
Alaw	114	390865	*Anglesey*
Cefni	114	445775	*Anglesey*
Cwmstradllyn	124	563445	*S.W. Blaenau Ffestiniog*
Llyn Cwellyn	115	560550	*S.E. Caernarvon*
Llyn Traffwll	114	325770	*Anglesey*

WEST WALES WATER DIVISION
Vicarage Hill, Aberaeron, Dyfed

	Map	Ref	General location
Llyn Craig-y-Pistyll	135	722857	*N.E. Aberystwyth*
Llyn Egnant	135	793671	*S.E. Aberystwyth*
Llyn Llygad Rheidol	135	792877	*N.E. Aberystwyth*
Llys-y-Fran	158	037250	*N.E. Haverfordwest*
Preseli or Rosebush	158	065295	*N.E. Haverfordwest*

WYE RIVER DIVISION
4 St. John Street, Hereford HR1 2NE

	Map	Ref	General location
Caban Coch	147	915635	*nr. Rhayader*
Claerwen	147	855652	*S.W. Rhayader*
Craig Goch	147	897695	*nr. Rhayader*
Dol-y-Mynach	147	905615	*nr. Rhayader*
Pen-y-Garreg	147	902675	*nr. Rhayader*

WREXHAM & EAST DENBIGHSHIRE WATER COMPANY
21 Egerton Street, Wrexham LL11 1ND

	Map	Ref	General location
Cae Llwyd	117	269478	*S.W. Wrexham*
Llyn Cyfynwy	117	216547	*N.W. Wrexham*
Nant-y-Frith	117	243532	*N.W. Wrexham*
Pendinas	117	235518	*W. Wrexham*
Penycae	117	266453	*S.W. Wrexham*
Ty Mawr	117	275480	*S.W. Wrexham*

SEVERN TRENT WATER AUTHORITY
LAKE VYRNWY UNIT
Llanwddyn, Oswestry, Salop SY10 0NA

	Map	Ref	General location
Lake Vyrnwy	125	990213	*S.W. Oswestry*

Apply first to the Authority for a permit needed to visit this reservoir.

Tourist Information

Symbols:

🛏 Bed booking reservation service operates for a small charge.

* Regional Head Office.

N Open all the year round.

E Open at Easter and from Spring Bank Holiday to September.

S Open July and August only.

Office opening hours are generally from 10.00 – 18.00 daily but there are a few local variations.

North Wales

Colwyn Bay, *Clwyd*
North Wales Tourism Council, Glan-y-don Hall, Civic Centre. Tel. (0492) 56881. (Written enquiries and bed bookings only.)
🛏 N *

Betws-y-Coed, *Gwynedd*
Wales Tourist Office. Tel. (06902) 426. 🛏 N

Blaenau Ffestiniog, *Gwynedd*
Snowdonia National Park and Wales Tourist Centre, High Street. Tel. (076 681) 360. 🛏 E

Caernarfon, *Gwynedd*
Wales Tourist Office, Slate Quay. Tel. (0286) 2232. 🛏 E

Colwyn Bay, *Clwyd*
Information Office, Prince of Wales Theatre. Tel. (0492) 30478. E

Colwyn Bay Hotels and Guest Houses and Wales Tourist Office. Tel. (0492) 55719 or 56044. 🛏 E

Conwy, *Gwynedd*
Snowdonia National Park and Wales Tourist Office, Castle Street. Tel. (049263) 2248. 🛏 E

Holyhead, *Gwynedd*
Wales Tourist Office, Marine Square, Salt Island Approach. Tel. (0407) 2622. 🛏 E

Holywell, *Clwyd*
Tourist Information Centre, A55. Opening summer 1978. 🛏 S

Llanberis, *Gwynedd*
Snowdonia National Park and Wales Tourist Centre, c/o The Community Centre, Lakeside. Tel. (028682) 765. 🛏 E

Llandudno, *Gwynedd*
Information Centre, Chapel Street. Tel. (0492) 76413. N

Information Kiosk, North Promenade. Tel. (0492) 76572. S

Information Office, Arcadia Theatre. Tel. (0492) 76413. Ext. 264. S

Llangollen, *Clwyd*
Wales Tourist Office, Town Hall. Tel. (0978) 860828. N

Llanrwst, *Gwynedd*
Snowdonia National Park Countryside Centre, Glan-y-Borth. Tel. (0492) 640604. N

Menai Bridge, Isle of Anglesey, *Gwynedd*
Isle of Anglesey Tourist Association Information Centre, Coed Cyrnol. Tel. (0248) 712626. N

Pentrefoelas, *Clwyd*
Wales Tourist Office, c/o Post Office. Tel. (06905) 640. S

Porthmadog, *Gwynedd*
Wales Tourist Office at Festiniog Railway Station. Tel. (0766) 2981. N

Prestatyn, *Clwyd*
Prestatyn Publicity Office, c/o Council Offices, Nant Hall Road. Tel. (07456) 2484. E

Pwllheli, *Gwynedd*
Personal callers to Wales Tourist Office, Station Square, Pwllheli, and letters of enquiry to Wales Tourist Office, c/o Town Hall. Tel. (0758) 3330. S

Rhyl, *Clwyd*
Wales Tourist Office, Information Bureau, Promenade. Tel. (0745) 55068. E
Town Hall Information Bureau. Tel. (0745) 31515. N

Whittington, *Salop.*
Tourist Information Centre, Babbinswood, near Oswestry. Tel. Whittington Castle 4888.

Wrexham, *Clwyd*
Tourist Information Centre, Guildhall Car Park, Town Centre. Tel. (0978) 57845. E

Mid Wales

Machynlleth, *Powys*
For Caravan and Camping Pitches in Mid Wales. Tel. Machynlleth (0654) 2727. S
Mid Wales Tourism Council, Owain Glyndwr Centre. Tel. (0654) 2401 or 2653. N *

Aberaeron, *Dyfed*
Tourist Information Centre, Harbour Car Park, Market Street. Tel. (054570) 602. E

Aberdovey, *Gwynedd*
Snowdonia National Park and Wales Tourist Centre, The Wharf. Tel. (065472) 321. E

Aberystwyth, *Dyfed*
Wales Tourist Office, The Seafront, Tel. (0970) 612125. E

Ceredigion District Council Offices, Park Avenue. Tel. (0970) 617911. Mon.–Fri. only. N

Bala, *Gwynedd*
Snowdonia National Park and Wales Tourist Centre, High Street. Tel. (06782) 367. E

Barmouth, *Gwynedd*
Barmouth Publicity Bureau and Wales Tourist Office, The Promenade. Tel. (0341) 280787. E

Builth Wells, *Powys*
Wales Tourist Office, Groe Car Park. Tel. (09822) 3307. E

Cardigan, *Dyfed*
Wales Tourist Office, The Market Place. Tel. (0239) 3230. E

Dinas Mawddwy, *Gwynedd*
Local information from Meirion Mill. Tel. (06504) 311. E

Dolgellau, *Gwynedd*
Snowdonia National Park and Wales Tourist Centre, The Bridge. Tel. (0341) 422888. E

Harlech, *Gwynedd*
Snowdonia National Park and Wales Tourist Centre, High Street. Tel. (076673) 658. E

Llandrindod Wells, *Powys*
Wales Tourist Office, Town Hall Gardens. Tel. (0597) 2600. N

Llanidloes, *Powys*
Wales Tourist Office, Great Oak Street. Tel. (05512) 2605. E

Machynlleth, *Powys*
Wales Tourist Office, Owain Glyndwr Centre. Tel. (0654) 2401. N

Newtown, *Powys*
Wales Tourist Office, Central Car Park. Tel. (0686) 25580. E

Ponterwyd, *Dyfed*
Local information from Llywernog Silver Lead Mine. Tel. (097085) 620. E

Rhayader, *Powys*
Wales Tourist Office, West Street. Tel. (059782) 591. E

Tregaron, *Dyfed*
Local information from A.T.O.M., The Square. Tel. (08744) 415. E

Tywyn, *Gwynedd*
Tywyn Publicity Office, Neptune Road. Tel. (0654) 710070. E

Welshpool, *Powys*
Wales Tourist Office, Vicarage Garden Car Park. Tel. (0938) 2043. N

South Wales

Carmarthen, *Dyfed*
South Wales Tourism Council, Darkgate. Tel. (0267) 7557. Telex 48286. N *

Aberavon, *West Glamorgan*
Afan District Council Offices. Tel. Port Talbot (06396) 3141. N

Abercraf, *Powys*
Tourist Information Centre, Dan-yr-Ogof Caves. Tel. (063977) 284. N

Abergavenny, *Gwent*
Wales Tourist Board and Brecon Beacons National Park Information Centre, 2 Lower Monk Street. Tel. (0873) 3254. E

Barry, *South Glamorgan*
Vale of Glamorgan Borough Council, Woodlands Road. Tel. 730311. N

Brecon, *Powys*
Wales Tourist Board Information Centre, Market Car Park. Tel. (0874) 2485. E

Brecon Beacons National Park, 7 Glamorgan Street. Tel. (0874) 2763. E

Brecon Beacons Mountain Centre, near Libanus, Brecon LD3 8ER. Tel. (0874) 3366. N

Broad Haven, *Pembrokeshire, Dyfed*
Pembrokeshire Coast National Park, Countryside Unit, Car Park. Tel. (043783) 412. E

Caerphilly, *Mid Glamorgan*
Tourist Information Centre, Twyn Car Park. Tel. (0222) 863378. E

Cardiff, *South Glamorgan*
Wales Tourist Board Information Centre, Castle Street. Tel. (0222) 27281. N
Tourist Information, Post House Hotel, Eastern Avenue. Tel. (0222) 750121. N

Carmarthen, *Dyfed*
Wales Tourist Board Information Centre, Old Bishops' Palace, Abergwili. E

Cwmbran, *Gwent*
Torfaen District Council, 42 Gwent Square. Tel. (06333) 67411. N

Fishguard, *Pembrokeshire, Dyfed*
Wales Tourist Board and Pembrokeshire Coast National Park Centre, Town Hall. Tel. (0348) 873484. ⊨ E

Haverfordwest, *Pembrokeshire, Dyfed*
Wales Tourist Board and Pembrokeshire Coast National Park Information Centre, 40 High Street. Tel. (0437) 3110. ⊨ E

Hay-on-Wye, *Powys*
Cinema Bookshop, Richard Booth Bookshop. Tel. (04972) 322. N

Kilgetty, *Pembrokeshire, Dyfed*
Wales Tourist Board and Pembrokeshire Coast National Park Information Centre, Kingsmoor Common. Tel. (0834) 813672/3. ⊨ N

Llandovery, *Dyfed*
Brecon Beacons National Park, Central Car Park, Broad Street. Tel. (0550) 20693. E

Merthyr Tydfil, *Mid Glamorgan*
Callers: Merthyr Borough Council, Technical College Car Park. Telephone enquiries to: John Stoker, Sports and Leisure Centre. Tel. Merthyr Tydfil 71491. N

Monmouth, *Gwent*
Wales Tourist Board Information Centre, c/o Nelson Museum. Tel. (0600) 3899. ⊨ E

Pembroke, *Pembrokeshire, Dyfed*
Pembrokeshire Coast National Park, Drill Hall, Main Street. Tel. (06463) 2148. E

Penarth, *South Glamorgan*
Information Office, West House. Tel. Penarth 707201. E

Porthcawl, *Mid Glamorgan*
Wales Tourist Board Information Centre, Old Police Station, John Street. Tel. (065671) 6637. ⊨ E

Raglan, *Gwent*
Wales Tourist Board Information Centre, Pen-y-clawdd Service Area. ⊨ N

St. David's, *Pembrokeshire, Dyfed*
Wales Tourist Board Information Centre, Car Park, High Street. Tel. (043788) 747. ⊨ E

National Park Centre, City Hall. Tel. (043788) 392. E

Swansea, *West Glamorgan*
Upper Killay Wales Tourist Board Information Centre, Fairwood Common. Tel. (0792) 7671/60. ⊨ E

Tourist Information Centre, Guildhall Kiosk, Swansea Guildhall. Tel. (0792) 50821. N

Wales Tourist Board Information Centre, Crumlin Burrows, Jersey Marine. Tel. (0792) 462403 or 462498. ⊨ E

Tourist Information Centre, Oystermouth Square, The Mumbles. Tel. (0792) 61302. ⊨ E

Talgarth, *Powys*
Tourist Information Centre, Bruton House, High Street. Tel. (087481) 586. N

Tenby, *Pembrokeshire, Dyfed*
South Pembrokeshire District Council and Pembrokeshire Coast National Park, Guild Hall, The Norton. Tel. (0834) 2402. (South Pembs.) or (0834) 3510 (Nat. Park). N

Tintern, *Gwent*
Wales Tourist Board Information Centre, Abbey Car Park. Tel. (02918) 431. ⊨ N

Treffgarne, *Haverfordwest, Dyfed*
Tourist Information Centre, Nant-y-Coy Mill. Tel. (043787) 223. E

Usk, *Gwent*
Tourist Information Centre, Old Smithy Gallery, Maryport Street. Tel. (02913) 2207. N

British Tourist Authority

Overseas Offices

Argentina
British Tourist Authority
Av. Cordoba 645 P. 2°
1054 Buenos Aires
Tel. 392-9955

Australia
British Tourist Authority
171 Clarence Street
Sydney N.S.W. 2000
Tel. 29-8627

Belgium
British Tourist Authority
23 Place Rogierplein 23
1000 Brussels
Tel. 02/219.04.83

Brazil
British Tourist Authority
Avenida Ipiranga 318-A, 12° Andar, conj. 1201
01046 Sao Paulo = SP
Tel. 257-1834

Canada
British Tourist Authority
151 Bloor Street West
Suite 460
Toronto, Ontario M5S IT3
Tel. (416) 925-6326

Denmark
British Tourist Authority (BTA)
Møntergade 5
1116 Copenhagen K
Tel. (01) 12 07 93

France
British Tourist Authority
6 Place Vendome
75001-Paris
Tel. 296 35 52

Germany
British Tourist Authority
Neue Mainzer Str. 22
6000 Frankfurt a.M.
Tel. (0611) 25 20 22

Holland
British Tourist Authority
Leidseplein 5
Amsterdam
Tel. (020) 23 46 67

Italy
British Tourist Authority
Via S. Eufemia 5
00187 Rome
Tel. 6784998 or 6785548

Japan
British Tourist Authority
Tokyo Club Building
3-2-6 Kasumigaseki
Chiyoda-ku, Tokyo 100
Tel. 581-3603

Mexico
British Tourist Authority
Rio Tiber 103 - 6 piso
Mexico 5 D.F.
Tel. 511.39.27 or 514.93.56

New Zealand
British Tourist Authority
Box 3655
Wellington
Tel. 843-223

Norway
British Tourist Authority
Postboks 1781 Vika
Oslo 1
Tel. (02) 41 18 49

South Africa
British Tourist Authority
Union Castle Building
36 Loveday Street
PO Box 6256
2000 Johannesburg
Tel. 838 1881

Spain
British Tourist Authority
Torre de Madrid 6/4
Plaza de España
Madrid 13
Tel. 241 13 96 or 248 65 91

Sweden
British Tourist Authority
For visitors: Malmskillnadsg
42 1st floor
For mail: Box 40 097
S–103 42 Stockholm 40
Tel. 08 – 21 83 64

Switzerland
British Tourist Authority
Limmatquai 78
8001 Zurich
Tel. 01 / 47 42 77 + 97

USA
680 Fifth Avenue
New York NY 10019
Tel. (212) 581–4708

612 South Flower Street
Los Angeles CA 90017
Tel. (213) 623–8196

John Hancock Center (Suite 2450)
875 North Michigan Avenue
Chicago IL 60611
Tel. (312) 787–0490

Suite 2115
Mercantile Commerce Building
1712 Commerce Street
Dallas TX 75201
Tel. (214) 748–2279

List of addresses of organisations mentioned in this booklet.

Central Electricity Generating Board, North Western Region, Europa House, Bird Hall Lane, Cheadle Heath, Stockport SK3 0XA.

Countryside Commission, Wales Office, 8 Broad Street, Newtown, Powys.

Forestry Commission, Churchill House, Churchill Way, Cardiff, S. Glamorgan.

Forestry Commission, Victoria House, Victoria Terrace, Aberystwyth, Dyfed.

National Trust, 22 Alan Road, Llandeilo, Dyfed. (South Wales Office.)

National Trust, Dinas, Betws-y-Coed, Gwynedd. (North Wales Office.)

Nature Conservancy Council, Penrhos Road, Bangor, Gwynedd.

Royal Society for the Protection of Birds, Wales Office, 18 High Street, Newtown, Powys.

Welsh Water Authority, Cambrian Way, Brecon, Powys LD3 7HP

County Councils:

Write to County Planning Department at:

Clwyd: Shire Hall, Mold.

Dyfed: 40 Spilman Street, Carmarthen.

Glamorgan: *West:* Metropole Chambers, Salubrious Passage, Swansea. *Mid:* County Offices, Cardiff. *South:* City Hall, Cardiff.

Gwent: County Hall, Cwmbran.

Gwynedd: Maesincla, Caernarfon.

Powys: County Hall, Llandrindod Wells

District and borough Councils:

Aberconwy Borough Council, Town Hall, Llandudno, Gwynedd.

Alyn and Deeside District Council, Council Offices, Hawarden, Clwyd.

Torfaen Borough Council, Gwent House, Cwmbran, Gwent.

Cardiff City Council, City Hall, Cardiff, South Glamorgan.

Colwyn Borough Council, Civic Centre, Colwyn Bay, Clwyd.

Cynon Valley Borough Council, Town Hall, Aberdare, Mid Glamorgan.

Islwyn Borough Council, Council Offices, Pontllanfraith, Gwent.

Monmouth District Council, Town Hall, Abergavenny, Gwent.

Rhuddlan Borough Council, Council Offices, Russell House, Russell Road, Rhyl, Clwyd.

Rhymney Valley District Council, Council Offices, Park Road, Hengoed, Mid Glamorgan.

South Pembs. District Council, Llanion Park, South Pembrokeshire, Dyfed.

Vale of Glamorgan Borough Council, Town Hall, Barry, South Glamorgan.

Wrexham Maelor Borough Council, The Guildhall, Wrexham, Clwyd.

Caernarfon Town Council, Council Chambers, Institute Buildings, Caernarfon, Gwynedd.

National Park Authorities:

Brecon Beacons: Glamorgan Street, Brecon, Powys.

Pembrokeshire Coast: Information Service, County Offices, Haverfordwest, Dyfed.

Snowdonia: Yr Hen Ysgol, Maentwrog, Blaenau Ffestiniog, Gwynedd.

Written communications should NOT be sent to Information Offices of the National Parks, only to the three addresses given here.

For information about membership of Naturalists' Trusts write to:

Brecknock: E. Bartlett, Chapel House, Llechfaen, Brecon, Powys.

Glamorgan: Mrs. K. E. White, Pengwern, 104 Broadway, Cowbridge.

Gwent: Gwent Trust for Nature Conservation, c/o G. G. Cowburn, Usk College of Agriculture, Usk, Gwent.

North Wales: Miss Liz Moyle, 154 High Street, Bangor, Gwynedd.

West Wales: D. Saunders, 20 High Street, Haverfordwest.

For membership of the Ramblers Association write to:

The Ramblers Association, Welsh Council, Trem-y-Foel, Llandyrnog, Denbigh, Clwyd CL16 4HB.

Designed and published by Wales Tourist Board. All rights reserved. Copyright © 1978, Wales Tourist Board, High Street, Llandaff, Cardiff, Wales. CF5 2YZ. Telephone Cardiff (0222) 567701. Printed in Wales by A. McLay & Co., Ltd., Cardiff. 5th Edition ISBN. 0 900784 67 9